THE UNOFFICIAL GUIDE TO TRANSFORMERS 1980s THROUGH 1990s

by J. E. Alvarez

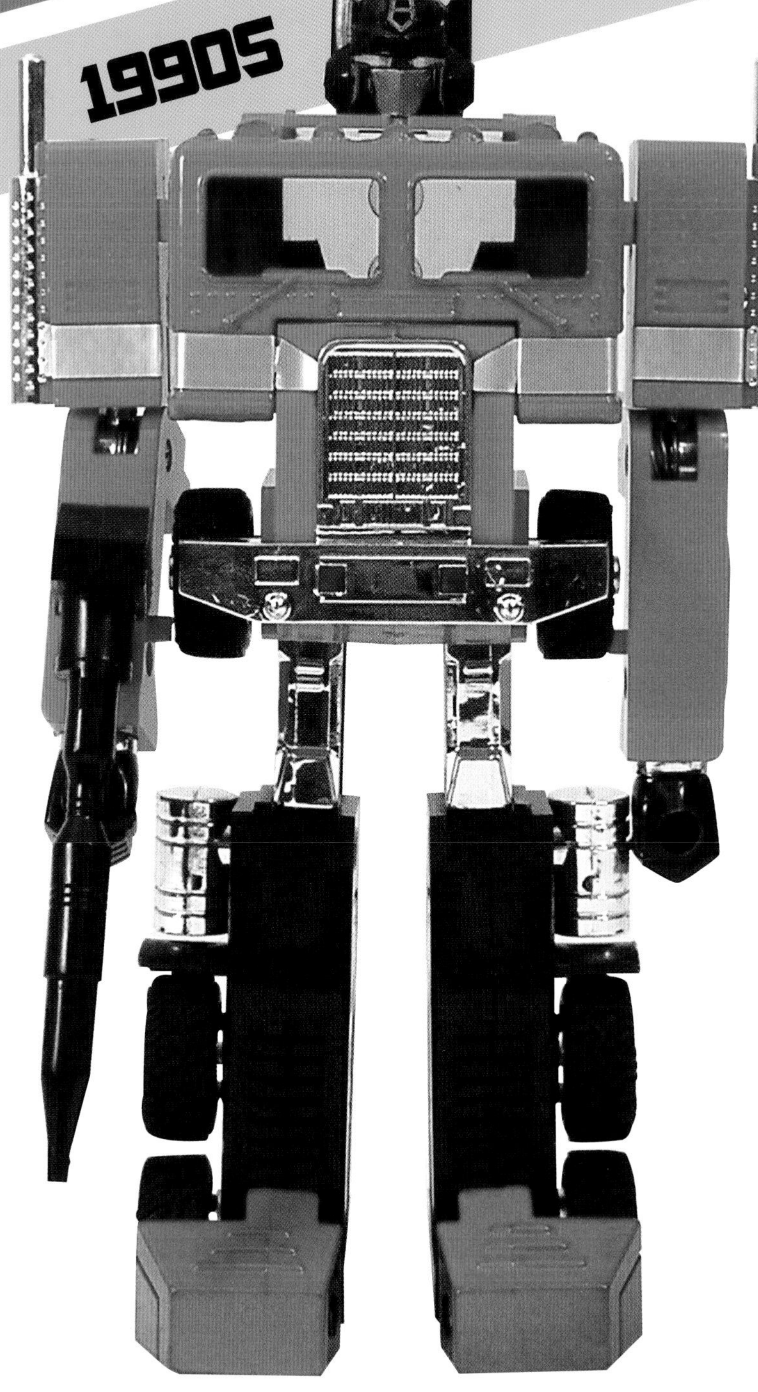

4880 Lower Valley Road • Atglen, PA 19310

Library of Congress Control Number: 2017935739

Designed by Molly Shields
Cover design by Justin Watkinson
Type set in Transformers Solid/Times New Roman

ISBN: 978-0-7643-5441-0
Printed in China

Published by Schiffer Publishing, Ltd.
4880 Lower Valley Road
Atglen, PA 19310
Phone: (610) 593-1777; Fax: (610) 593-2002
E-mail: Info@schifferbooks.com
Web: www.schifferbooks.com

I lovingly dedicate this latest edition to my beautiful wife Allana and our daughters, Casey and Maddie.

CONTENTS

ACKNOWLEDGMENTS

BIGBADTOYSTORE

Rarely in life does a project come together without the help of others. I am very happy to acknowledge the people who made this book possible.

From past editions I would like to recognize John Marshall for introducing me to the team at Schiffer Publishing, and Daniel Hodgkinson, George Hubert Jr., Ronald Bahr, Donovon Talley, and Robert T. Yee for allowing me to use items from their personal collections throughout this book.

Of significant importance is Scott Talis, owner of Play With This Toys and Collectibles. Scott imparted to me a great deal of knowledge regarding the collecting world. Many items from my personal collection passed through his hands first. Please visit his store (the original) Play With This Toys and Collectibles at 19 W. Park Ave., Merchantville, New Jersey, 08109, or call (856) 320-6163. Scott carries a plethora of collectibles from the 1960s through today.

From this edition I would like to thank two very special people who made my life a lot easier: Duron Land and Orson Christian. Duron and Orson took the time to dig out, transport, and photograph their collections. They are the heroes of this book, as much of my collection was packed up and in storage at the time. Without them this edition would not have been possible. If you are currently collecting please visit Orson's online store www.capturedprey.com, or visit his booth at any major Transformers convention. Duron did most of the photography for this book. He also hosts a podcast I tend to sit in on from time to time, www.tfylp.com. To see more of his photography please visit www.facebook.com/lightboxproductphotos.

Thank you to Morgan Colyer for trusting Orson and Duron (Yella Wolf Studios) to handle items from his collection. Morgan was kind enough to provide some excellent information and images of very rare figures. Please visit his website at www.iamratchet.com.

I would like to extend my last minute thanks to Chuck Liu of www.artfire2000.com. Chuck was nice enough to provide a magnitude of images after the manuscript was done and about to be handed in. Chuck deals primarily in rare and vintage Japanese Transformers.

I would also like to thank Chuck for introducing me to Ronen Kauffman, who has an extraordinary collection of Minicars. Ronen has spent many years amassing such a particular collection, and I thank him for taking the time to share it. Ronen lives with his wife and son in New Jersey. He collects vintage Transformers (and other toys, too), and produces Transformers-influenced toy art. Follow him on Instagram @myth_lab and learn more at www.toylab.info.

Also Erik Nelson for lending me items from his collection and assisting me with photography.

I would like to recognize Tony Preto from Tempting Toys for help with information and for selling me a great deal of my rare toys. For new and old toys his website is www.temptingcollectibles.com.

Special thanks to a man who is a personal hero of mine and a worthy friend, Mr. Joel Boblit of www.bigbadtoystore.com.

I'd like to thank the very patient people at Schiffer Publishing: from previous editions Jeff Snyder and Molly Higgins for editing and photography, and the Schiffer family for the opportunities these various books have provided me. And from this edition my editor Ian Robertson for all his hard work and for letting me tell him how it is.

Finally, I would like to thank my mother Gioconda, who bought me my first Transformer in 1984, at a K-Mart in New Jersey, and especially my wonderful wife Allana for putting up with my mess.

Before Transformers existed came Takara's Diaclone toy line. Here is the figure that would go on to become Transformers' Bluestreak alongside his Diaclone pilot. *Courtesy of Chuck Liu of artfire2000.com*

INTRODUCTION

What exactly is a Transformer? In most instances, a Transformer is a figure that through a series of adjustments or movements can have its form altered from a vehicle or animal into a bipedal robot. This concept of change is indicative to these first two decades of the Transformers brand. While some toys expanded the idea of what could and could not transform, and what form that alternate mode would take, the fundamental idea of change was present in each and every product.

The Transformers is a legacy brand which has transcended generations and will continue to do so. They are a staple of popular culture through their expressions in films, television, comic books, games, and licensed goods, but especially toys. With the expanding popularity and diversification of the brand, more and more people are exploring collecting the older toys at the center of the Transformers legacy. Since the first edition of this book the Internet has expanded, and with it vast sums of knowledge on every subject imaginable. Trying to find where to begin expanding your awareness of certain subjects can be daunting. This book is not intended to serve as a parts guide for each figure, but rather as an easy access, introductory guide into the first two decades of the Transformers brand. Pictured are examples of many of the toys released in the United States during the 1980s and 1990s, along with descriptions of their key features. Each chapter corresponds to a particular year of the brand unless noted on individual photographs. The final chapter features licensed goods produced during the aforementioned time.

Each chapter is arranged by year of release and provides a checklist of products. The prices listed in this book provide a reference on what certain items can cost. As more time passes from this book's printing these prices will obviously change. Generally, something is only worth what someone is willing to pay for it. The prices listed may at times conflict with the perceived value of an item based on individual preference, individual collector necessity, availability, and even location. To gather the suggested prices I consulted long time vintage toy dealers Tony Preto of Temptingcollectibles.com, Orson Christian of Capturedprey.com, and Morgan Colyer of iamratchet.com. I also took into account my own experience collecting over the past twenty-plus years, as well as researched prices via online auction sites. Online auction sites—the biggest being eBay—can sometimes have mitigating factors which can determine their final auction prices. Often online auction prices really depend on who is watching for a particular item on any

given day, versus who has the money at the time the item is available, versus the location of the item and shipping constraints. Prices for online auctions vary wildly, and I implore you to keep that in mind when doing your own research.

Briefly touched upon are examples of Transformer toys released in other countries. There are some examples of international toy and packaging variations, but the subject is too great to encompass into an easy access introductory guide. This has been covered in depth in *The Unofficial Guide to Japanese and International Transformers*. Also included are the first few years of Beast Wars, with all examples photographed in package as they first saw release in 1996. With Beast Wars being such a vast line of Transformers they have been covered extensively in *Beast Wars: An Unofficial Guide*.

This edition has allowed me to look back over the past fifteen-plus years since this book was first published and craft something very different from its two previous incarnations. Many of the original photographs have been replaced with new images featuring items in better condition, as well as providing more detailed information. Since the release of the live action Transformers films a tremendous amount of people have joined the collecting community. Many of those people were born in the new millennium, and to them I hope this guide provides a great starting point for collecting and learning about the first generation of Transformers. For those who grew up in the 1980s, I hope this book is an adequate pictorial reintroduction to your childhood, and to the legacy of the heroic Autobots and the evil Decepticons.

Purchased in 1984, from a K-Mart near Mt. Laurel, New Jersey, my first Transformers ever. *Courtesy of Gioconda E. Maglione*

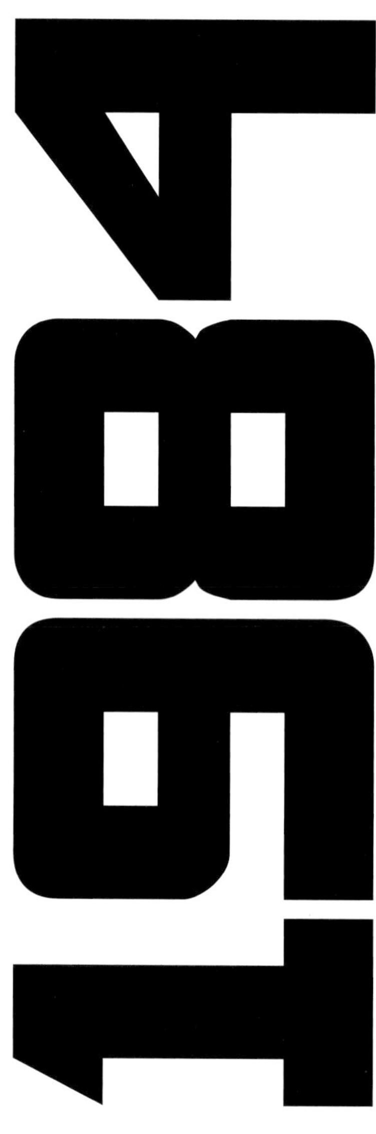

CHAPTER ONE

1984

The Transformers toy line officially began in 1984, and was first released in the United States by toy manufacturer Hasbro. However, leading up to their "official" creation was a series of toy lines made up of various figures who would eventually be repurposed and rebranded as some of the very first Transformers. These original sources included the Japanese Diaclone and Micro Change toy lines produced by Takara (now known as TakaraTomy). The Diaclone toy line began in 1980, with a series of futuristically themed transforming vehicles. By 1982, the line had transitioned to feature transforming robots with realistic alternate modes, such as sports cars and jet planes. In 1983, Takara released several of these later figures in the United States as part of a line called Diakron. These early US Takara releases included versions of what were to become Sunstreaker, Ironhide, and Trailbreaker. In 1983, Micro Change, an offshoot of Takara's Microman brand, debuted in Japan, featuring true-to-life sized transforming pistols, tape decks, and cassettes (such as Frenzy and Ravage), as well as pocket-sized cars (the precursor versions of the Autobot Minicars) that transformed into robots roughly two inches in size. The primary group of 1984 and 1985 Transformers figures were created from these two lines. Very little fiction existed for either of these toy lines: there were no factions, no good robot versus evil robot, and often the figures were assigned product numbers rather than actual names.

During the 1983 Tokyo Toy Show, and perhaps keenly aware of the success Tonka had with the release of the GoBots line that same year, Hasbro representatives were able to enter into a licensing agreement with Takara to create a singular brand around several of their existing Diaclone and Microman toys. Hasbro repurposed many of the figures, some using existing color applications (known in the industry as deco) and even Takara packaging art. While working in conjunction with Marvel Entertainment, which established much of the early fiction, Hasbro was able to create two factions of battling robots, faction symbols with color patterns, character names, backstories, and an overall brand bible. These became the foundation of everything we still see today in entertainment and toys.

In 1984, when The Transformers brand launched, with it came a wide assortment of toys, a cartoon series, and what was to become an ongoing comic book from Marvel. As is often the case with many new brands, product variations existed in packaging and on the figures, including the colors of plastics used in toy production, packaging variations, and in some extreme cases variations in the actual tooling of the toys. In several cases, as with the Decepticon jets or Soundwave's fists, these variations are of little interest to collectors. Explaining them would detract from this being an easy access guide. More often than not variations exist among international markets. These more blatant variants can often cost more due to their scarcity in the secondary collector market. Several of these variations (the most common) are showcased throughout this book, but for a wider view refer to the checklist featured in each chapter.

This was the start of what we know as Generation One.

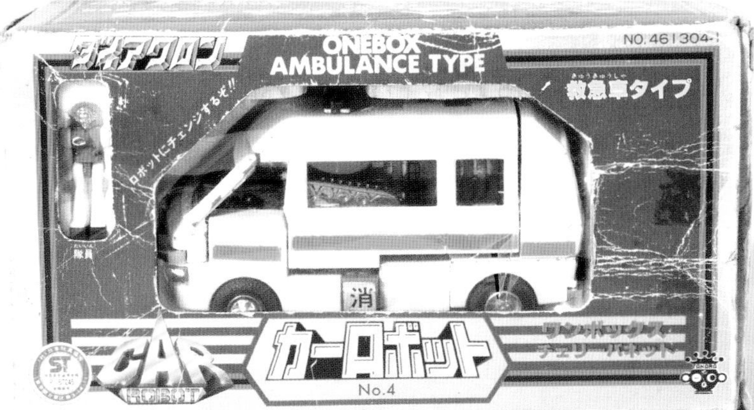

Diaclone "Ambulance Type" was the predecessor of Autobot Ratchet. *Courtesy of Chuck Liu of artfire2000.com*

The Diaclone figure Battle Convoy would go on to become the Autobot leader Optimus Prime. *Courtesy of Chuck Liu of artfire2000.com*

1984 CHECKLIST

Autobot Minicars (Carded)
Bumblebee (yellow body)
Bumblebee (red body)
Cliffjumper (yellow body)
Cliffjumper (red body)
Huffer
Windcharger
Brawn
Gears
*Bumper (on Cliffjumper card back)
(on Bumblebee card back)

Autobot Cars (Boxed)
Bluestreak
Hound
Ironhide
Jazz
Mirage
Prowl
Sideswipe
Sunstreaker
Trailbreaker
Wheeljack
Ratchet
Ratchet (with red cross on box art)

Autobot Leader (Boxed)
Optimus Prime (with silver Roller and large components)
Optimus Prime (with blue Roller and standard components)

Decepticon Cassettes (Carded)
Frenzy and Laserbeak
Rumble and Ravage

Decepticon Jets (Boxed)
Skywarp
Starscream
Thundercracker

Other Decepticons (Boxed)
Soundwave with Buzzsaw
Megatron

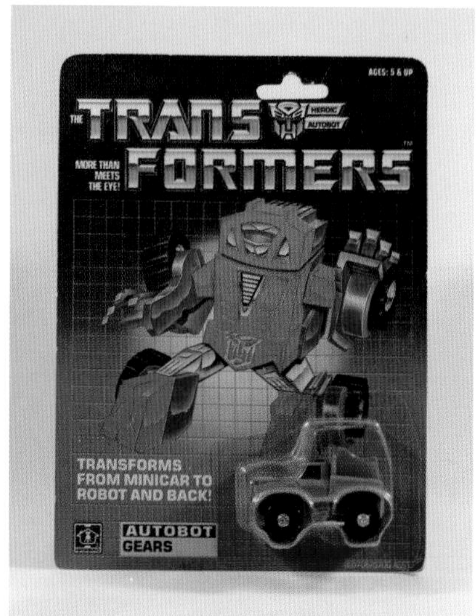

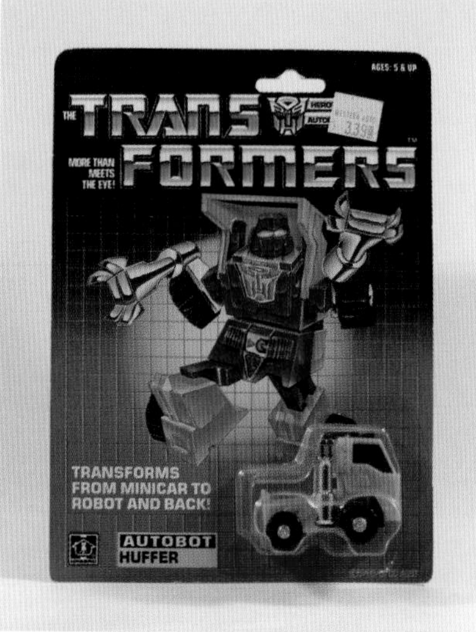

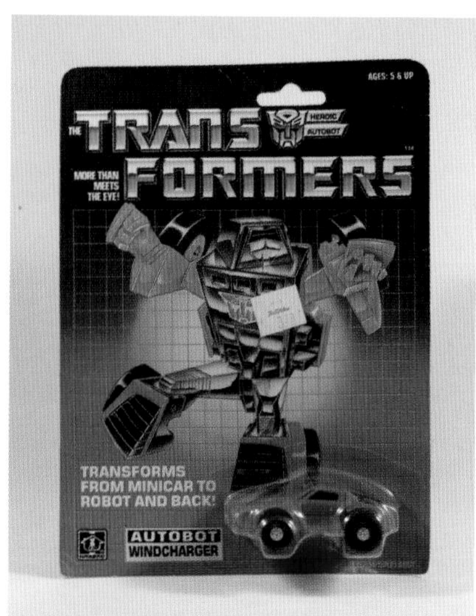

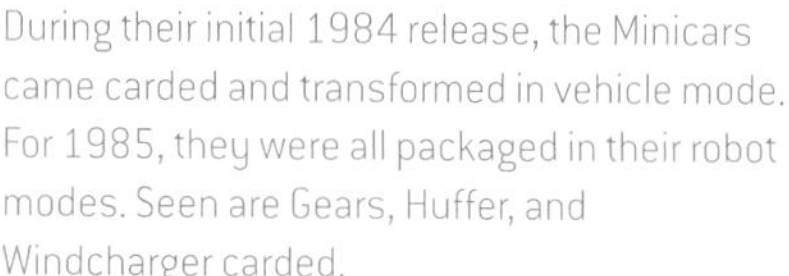
During their initial 1984 release, the Minicars came carded and transformed in vehicle mode. For 1985, they were all packaged in their robot modes. Seen are Gears, Huffer, and Windcharger carded.

For their Japanese release the following year, each Minicar came individually boxed with styrofoam inserts. *Courtesy of Ronen Kauffman of toylab.info*

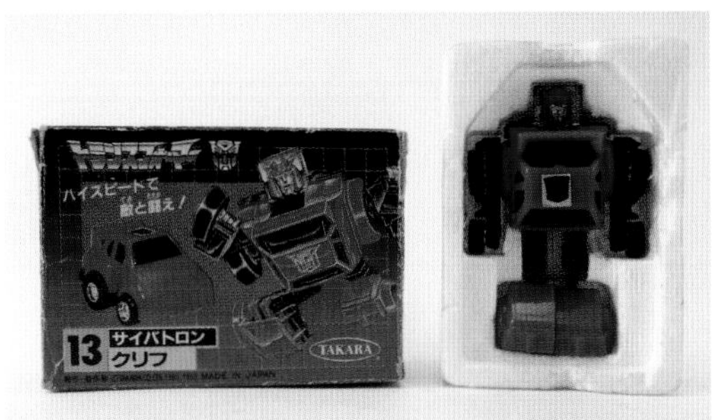

Yellow body Bumblebee carded. *Courtesy of Dan Hodgkinson*

Courtesy of Ronen Kauffman of toylab.info

(L to R) Windcharger, Huffer, Bumblebee, Gears, Cliffjumper, and Brawn. *Courtesy of Ronen Kauffman of toylab.info*

Seen here are the 1985 Minicars with rubsigns for comparison. *Courtesy of Ronen Kauffman of toylab.info*

Yellow body Cliffjumper. *Courtesy of Chuck Liu of artfire2000.com*

Given the moniker Bumblejumper by the fandom, it was not until the new millennium and the Dreamwave Transformers series of comic books that this character was officially brought into the fiction and named Bumper. This is the rarest Minicar released in North America. *Courtesy of Dan Hodgkinson*

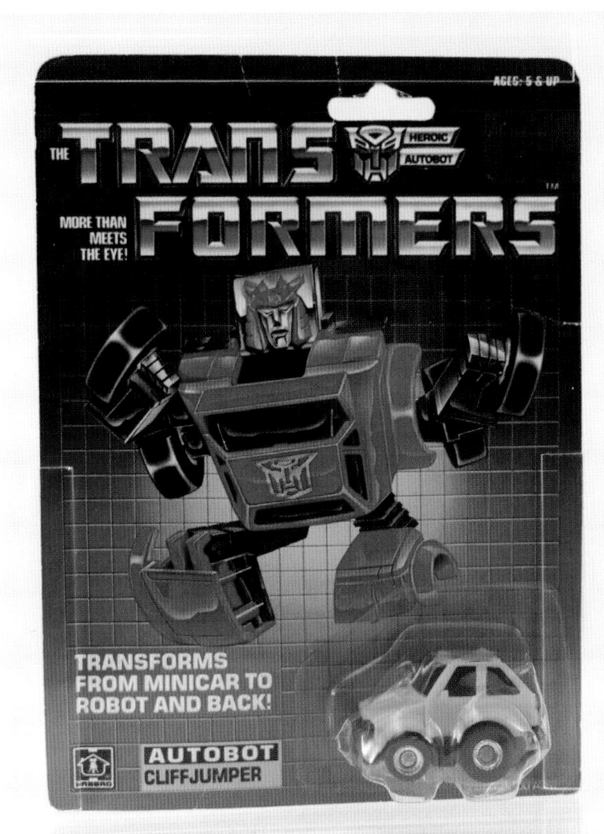

Because of the similarities to Bumblebee and Cliffjumper, this figure was released on Bumblebee and Cliffjumper card backs, but was a unique toy that was never advertised or officially named in the fiction. This item was most likely a production mistake on the part of the factory. *Courtesy of Ronen Kauffman of toylab.info*

Red body Bumblebee (1985 version with rubsign).

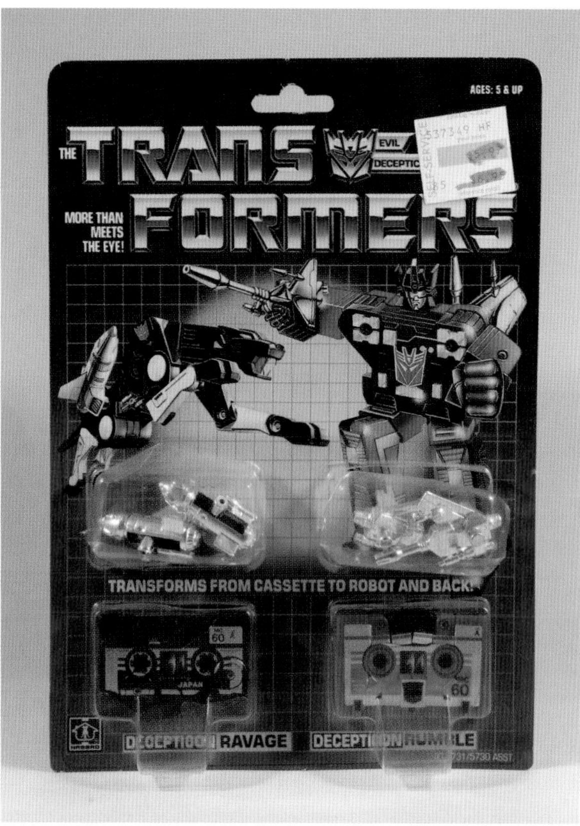

There are no discernible differences between the 1984 and 1985 carded versions of the Decepticon cassettes, which is why the 1984 versions are not shown. The only differences are the rubsigns on the figures. Seen here are Ravage and Rumble carded (1985 versions).

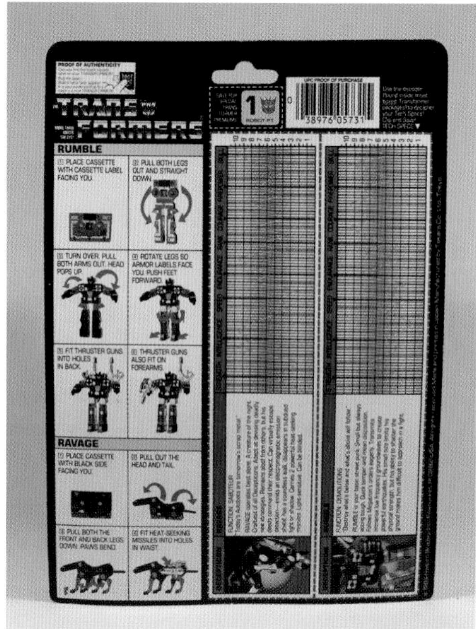

In Japan each character came with a number designation; eventually this numbering system was modified using a prefix. For example, C-54 and D-54 stood for Cybertron-54 or Destron-54. Cybertron was the Japanese name for Autobots, while Destron were the Decepticons. In Japan many carded figures initially came individually boxed. Seen here are Ravage and Laserbeak. *Courtesy of Ron Bahr*

Frenzy and Laserbeak carded (1985 versions). There is a neverending debate in the fandom: Is Rumble blue or red? Is Frenzy red or blue? In the television series Frenzy was red and Rumble was blue, but the toy colors were reversed. Throughout the years various figures of the two have been released, with the names swapping back and forth between red and blue.

Top: Rumble and Ravage. Bottom: Laserbeak (1985 version) and Frenzy.

Rumble and Ravage (1985 version).

Frenzy and Laserbeak.

The 1985/1986 plastic feet for Frenzy (left) compared to the original 1984 metal feet. Rumble had this same variation.

Collectors will pay a premium for vintage toys in the box, but more so for figures still sealed in the box. A sealed 1984 Jazz can sell between $500 and $1,200. Because this particular toy has been reissued several times by Hasbro and Takara, the price for the vintage piece has been driven down.

Although released in Japan a year later, here is a comparison between the Hasbro Hound (1984) and the Takara Hound (1985). *Courtesy of Chuck Liu of artfire2000.com*

A figure with the box can still fetch a premium, even if the box lacks the inserts. Windox boxes such as this Wheeljack will not raise the price as much as a non-window box, which is able to conceal missing inserts.

From l to r: Hound, Jazz (1985 version), Mirage, and Wheeljack. *Courtesy of Orson Christian of CapturedPrey.com*

From left to right are Hound, Wheeljack, Mirage, and Jazz. *Courtesy of Orson Christian of CapturedPrey.com*

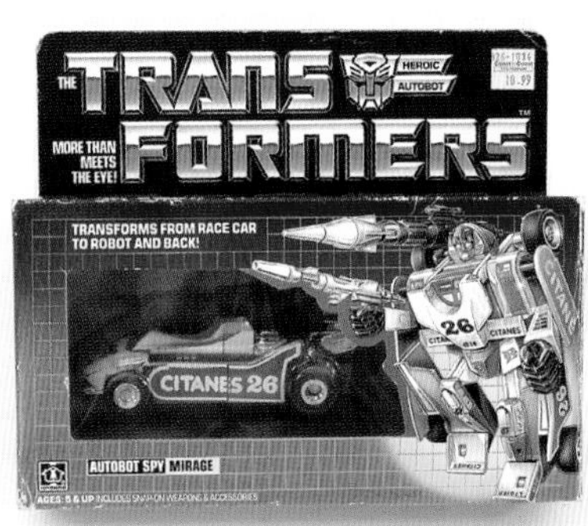

Courtesy of Chuck Liu of artfire2000.com

Sunstreaker (as of yet) has never been reissued. A sealed piece can sell for upwards of $600 to $1,200. *Courtesy of Dan Hodgkinson*

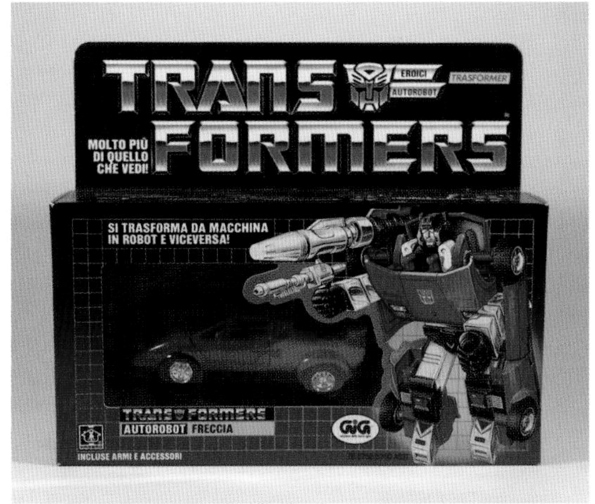

GiG was an Italian distribution company that licensed a deal with Hasbro to release the Transformers brand in their market. At times GiG would rename characters, such as this Sideswipe figure renamed Freccia. GiG released Transformers from the early 1980s until the mid-1990s. GiG items in Hasbro-inspired packaging will sell for several hundred dollars, but North American packaged items will always sell for several hundred dollars more, and at times a thousand dollars more. This item was released in 1985, and sealed can sell for $600–1,500.

From l to r: Sideswipe (1985 version), Sunstreaker, and Trailbreaker. *Courtesy of Orson Christian of CapturedPrey.com*

Takara released their original Transformers assortments each with a designated number. Later on the numbering system was modified, i.e., to C-44 or D-44. The C stood for the Cybertrons, which was the Takara name for Autobots, while the D stood for Destrons (Decepticons). *Courtesy of Chuck Liu of artfire2000.com*

Sunstreaker, Sideswipe, and Trailbreaker. *Courtesy of Orson Christian of CapturedPrey.com*

From l to r: Prowl, Bluestreak, Ironhide, and Ratchet. *Courtesy of Orson Christian of CapturedPrey.com*

From l to r: Ratchet, Bluestreak, Ironhide (1985 version), and Prowl. The 1984 figures set precedence in the way Transformers figures were released. While other toy lines, such as Masters of the Universe, used full unchanged repaints of figures sparingly due mostly to being human based, Hasbro could easily repaint a robot character, call it by another name, release it in the same assortment, and have it make sense. From 1984 to the present, often certain characters are repaints of another toy. Ratchet and Ironhide will usually share a mold. Starscream, Skywarp, and Thundercracker are usually all the same toy. Prowl, Bluestreak, and Smokescreen are all the same toy with some minor tweaks. *Courtesy of Orson Christian of CapturedPrey.com*

In 1984, Hasbro merged with rival toy company Milton Bradley, and by 1985, began using Milton Bradley's European distribution. Many of the figures released in Europe sport the Milton Bradley logo on the packaging. This trend continued into the early 1990s. Milton Bradley packaged Ratchet sealed can sell for $550–$1,000.

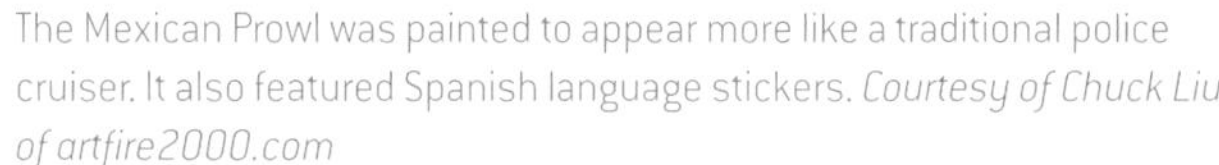

The Mexican Prowl was painted to appear more like a traditional police cruiser. It also featured Spanish language stickers. *Courtesy of Chuck Liu of artfire2000.com*

Prowl was released with several paint changes in Mexico. In a sealed box this item can range between $4,500 and $5,500. *Courtesy of Chuck Liu of artfire2000.com*

Skywarp and Thundercracker. Much like the rest of the 1984 line-up, these characters would become a staple of the franchise for the next thirty years.

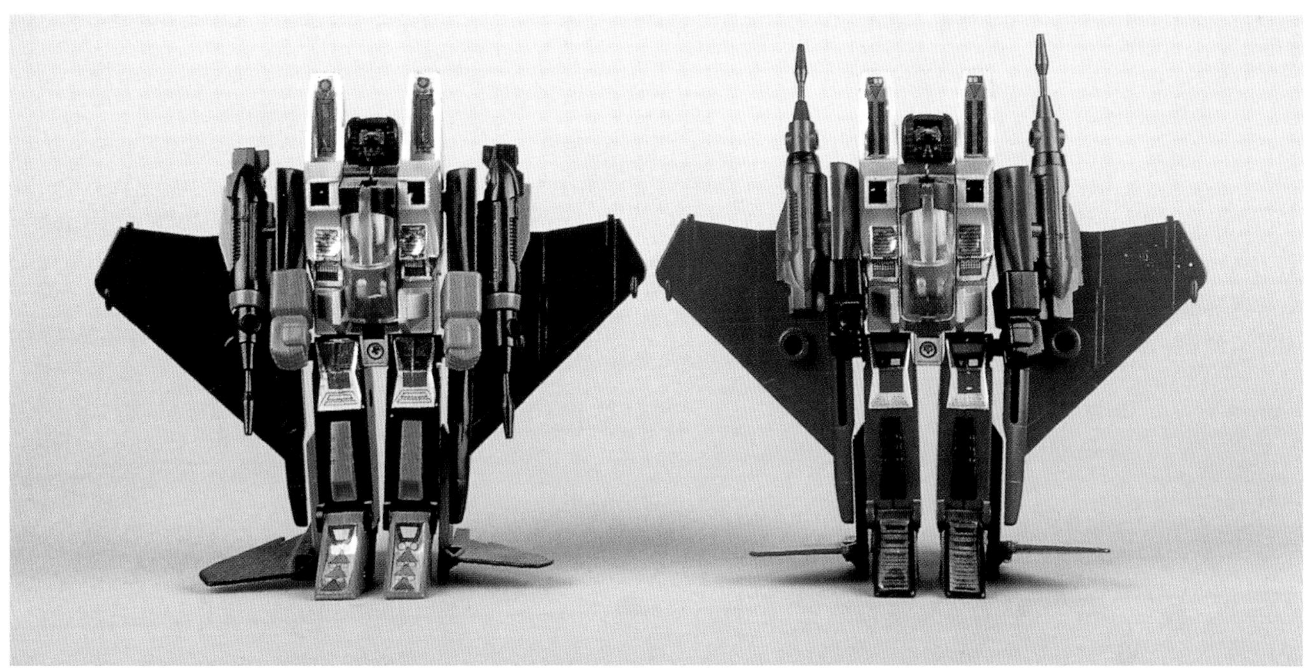

Starscream. Decepticon jets are referred to as Seekers. These figures came with two sets of missiles: long missiles for the robot mode and shorter missiles for the vehicle mode. Unlike many Transformers produced today, many of these early figures had additional accessories, such as hands, missiles, and swords, which could not fold into the vehicle form. Many of these accessories tend to get lost. Most modern figures have all weapons hide or become part of the vehicle mode so nothing is left out. *Courtesy of George Hubert*

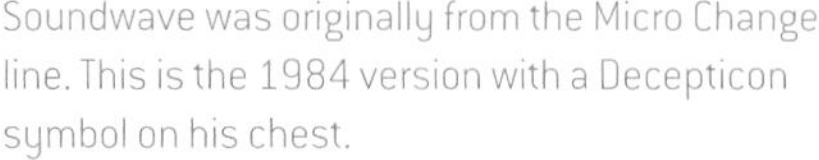

Soundwave was originally from the Micro Change line. This is the 1984 version with a Decepticon symbol on his chest.

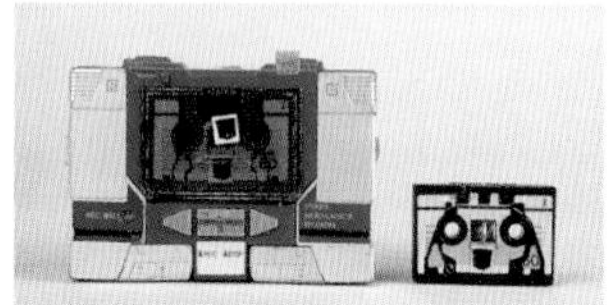

For comparison, here is the 1985 Soundwave with the Decepticon sticker replaced by a rubsign. Soundwave came with a Laserbeak repaint named Buzzsaw. This was the only way to obtain the Buzzsaw figure from Hasbro.

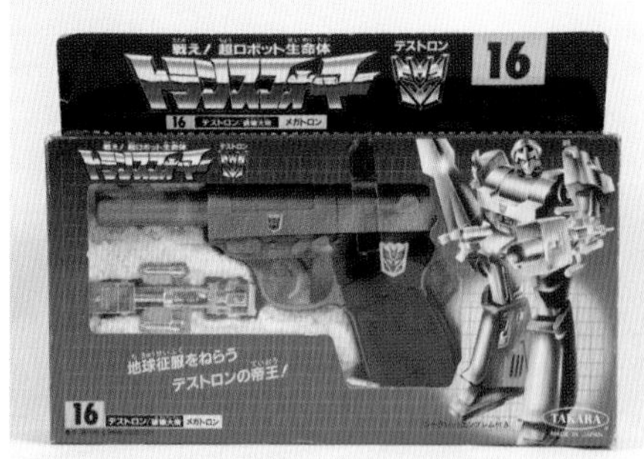

Megatron's Japanese packaging. *Courtesy of Chuck Liu of artfire2000.com*

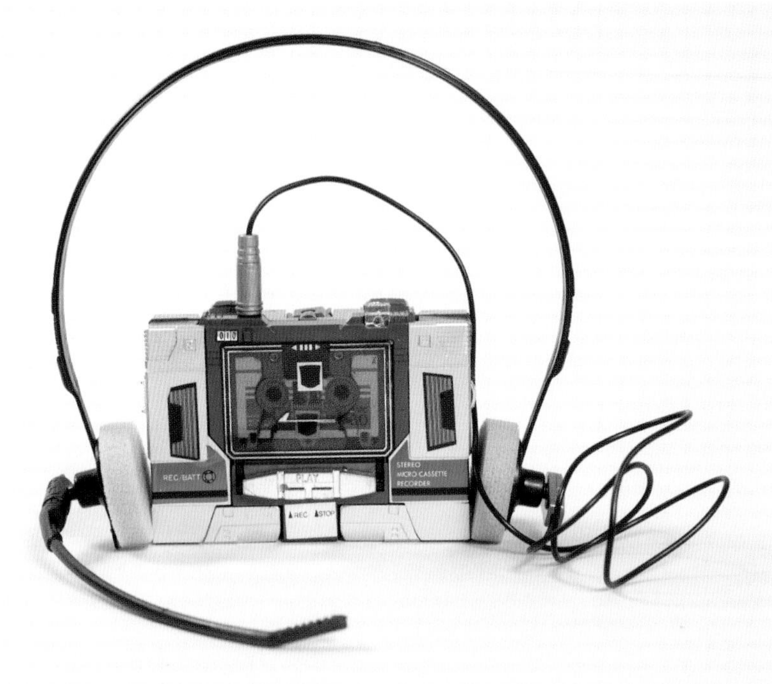

Megatron, leader of the Decepticons. While many 1984 and 1985 figures were reissued in North America at the start of the millennium, current US gun laws prevent Megatron from being reissued due to his striking resemblance to a Walther P-38. He was reissued in Japan several times.

The Micro Change and Takara releases of Soundwave came with a set of headphones to add to the concept of robots in disguise. *Courtesy of Chuck Liu of artfire2000.com*

Takara's Megatron figure did not come chromed. In the original release it did come with a chromed sword and blaster. The scope, silencer, and stalk were released with various later versions. The right arm of this first Megatron also lacked the piece to attach the scope. The first Megatron by Takara also came with dark blue on the inside of the legs instead of red. *Courtesy of Chuck Liu of artfire2000.com*

The Takara Megatron also came with an additional feature which the Hasbro version did not: when in gun mode Megatron could actually fire pellets (seen right in red). Seen here is the 1986 Takara release of Megatron from the Goodbye Megatron Gift Set from 1986. *Courtesy of Orson Christian of CapturedPrey.com*

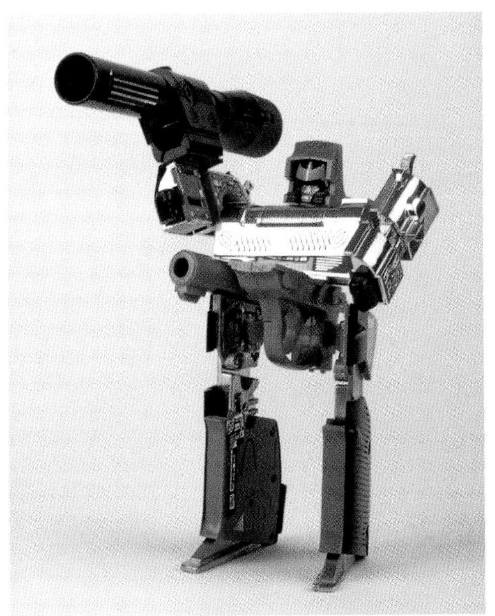

The Megatron toy was originally called Gun Robo–P38 and came from the Microman toy line.

The toy had the option of attaching the scope, silencer, and stalk to create a larger handgun as seen in the television series and comic books.

Unlike many of the other figures from the time, Megatron's accessories could combine into a stand-alone canon. This canon was never seen in the fiction, nor was his silver blaster.

Here it is seen without the accessories attached.

The Optimus Prime toy was first released as Battle Convoy in the Diaclone line. Multiple color variations and slight remoldings exist on this figure. This easy access guide will highlight the more common ones.

A variation from several years later that was manufactured and released in France, this red foot Optimus Prime is particularly rare. A sealed sample could sell for $12,000–$15,000+. *Courtesy of Chuck Liu of artfire2000.com*

Optimus Prime's trailer transformed into a battle station or repair bay. Seen on the center of the trailer in blue is his companion drone, Roller.

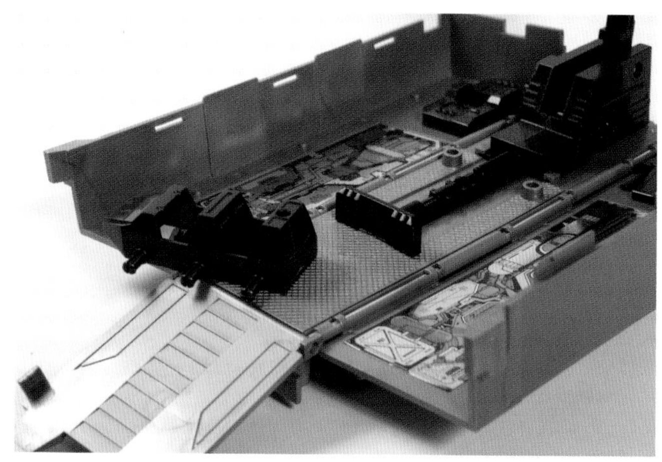

Takara released multiple variations of the Optimus Prime trailer. Seen here is one of the earliest versions which came with the Diaclone Battle Convoy super launcher. *Courtesy of Chuck Liu of artfire2000.com*

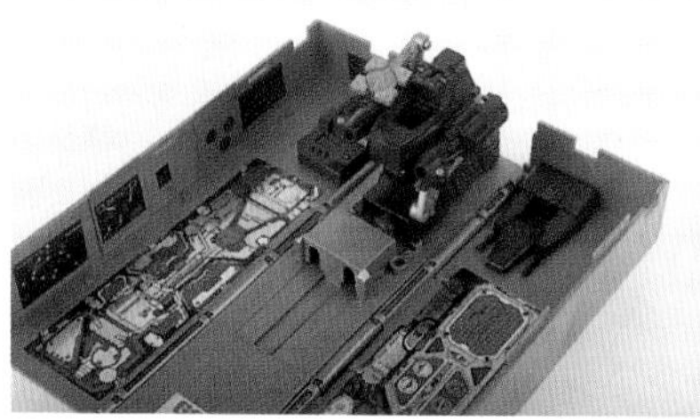

The first Optimus Prime figures released came with a silver Roller, silver missiles, and a silver launcher in the trailer. This version also had extra large fists, a large blaster, and a unique gas pump for Roller. Within the fandom this is commonly known as the bubble fist variant.

The second release trailer's interior shows the black launcher.

Here is a close-up of the large (sometimes referred to as bubble) hands and blaster for the Optimus Prime figure that came with the silver roller. *Courtesy of Ronen Kauffman of toylab.info*

With a sealed Optimus Prime it can be almost impossible to tell whether one has a figure with the large or regular-sized hands. The only discernible difference can be seen on the trailer, with small slits or "vents" running along the top and bottom of the center stripes. Subsequent Optimus Primes and all reissues did not come with these slits. This is the common release of the figure. Despite being reissued numerous times, an Optimus Prime figure sealed in a mint box can sell for upwards of $7,000.

Also released in 1985 by Takara but shown for comparison is the VSX Gift Set of Optimus Prime and Megatron. This had a somewhat limited product run in Japan. A sealed set (should it ever surface) will most likely range between $20,000 and $25,000. *Courtesy of Chuck Liu of artfire2000.com*

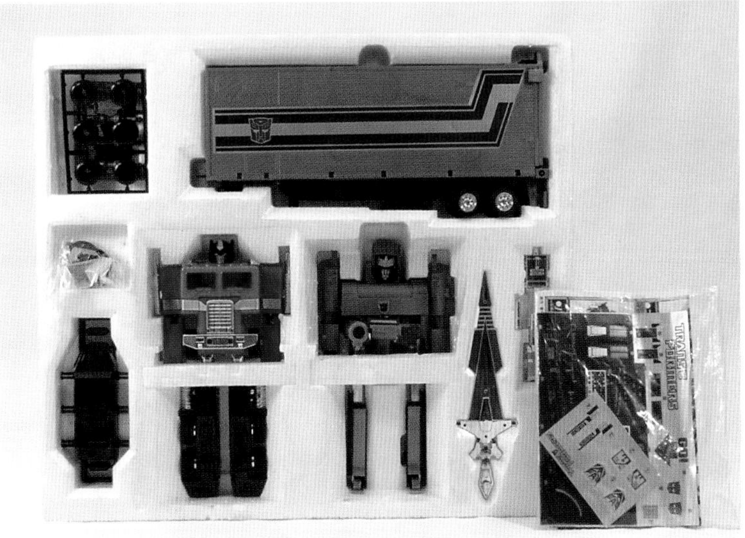

The Takara version of Optimus Prime from 1985. *Courtesy of Chuck Liu of artfire2000.com*

MINICARS

Before there were unified distribution plans and marketing offices in every country pushing out a core concept, character, color palette, and package design, variations were extremely prominent in many brands of the 1980s. Here is a focused look at various Mini-Car variations from around the world. Minicars were an easy entry point for Transformers product to be released worldwide because of their lower price points. Many markets during the 1980s (and even to this day) could not handle the larger scale figures due to local economies. Because of this lack of a collected marketing plan, local offices were able to create figures with new names, colors, and even fiction around them.

The pre-Transformers era Micro Change Bumper in red. This red version was never released under the Transformers brand. *Courtesy of Ronen Kauffman of toylab.info*

What became known as the Minicars in the Transformers line began as part of Takara's Micro Change toy line in Japan.

Micro Change Bumblebee in red. *Courtesy of Ronen Kauffman of toylab.info*

Pre-Transformers Micro Change Bumper in yellow. *Courtesy of Ronen Kauffman of toylab.info*

Micro Change Cliffjumper in red. While many of the Transformers color schemes were based on existing Micro Change or Diaclone colors, at times changes were made to the stickers. Some stickers were omitted altogether and replaced with Autobot and/or Decepticon faction symbol stickers. *Courtesy of Ronen Kauffman of toylab.info*

Micro Change Gears. *Courtesy of Ronen Kauffman of toylab.info*

In parts of Europe, Joustra (which was owned by Ceji) licensed Diaclone toys from Takara. At the time of this particular item's release, Takara was already producing figures under the Transformers label for Hasbro, so several Diaclone figures released by Joustra came with Transformers faction stickers or full Transformers sticker sheets. *Courtesy of Ronen Kauffman of toylab.info*

These color variants were released in Argentina, most likely during 1985. Produced by a company called Antex, they can range from $80 to $100 each carded.

Courtesy of Ronen Kauffman of toylab.info

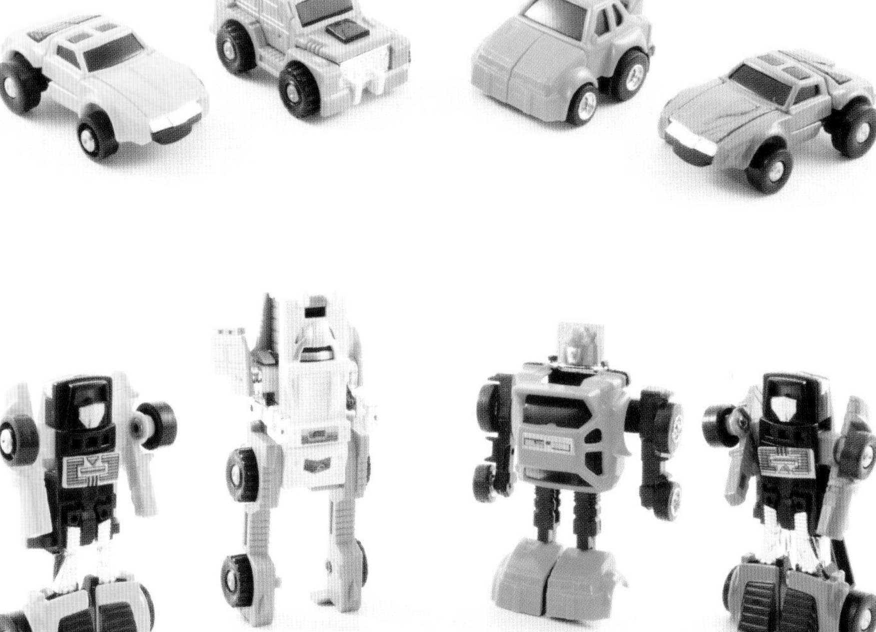

From l to r: Windcharger (yellow), Brawn, Cliffjumper, and Windcharger (blue). The Brawn was released in Brazil under the name Jipe and his colors are very similar to Outback. *Courtesy of Orson Christian of CapturedPrey.com*

Also produced by Antex. *Courtesy of Ronen Kauffman of toylab.info*

Cliffjumper (left) and Bumblebee (right). *Courtesy of Ronen Kauffman of toylab.info*

Brawn and Windcharger from Venezuela, released in 1989. The colors are similar to their 1984 versions, but the reverse of the card backs did not have any printing whatsoever. The front of the cards featured similar graphics to the Argentina versions.

Several of the Minicars were also released in colors similar to their North American counterparts. Seen here is the red body Bumblebee from Argentina. The back of the card shows Cliffjumper, Bumblebee, and Windcharger in their 1984 colors, but those could have been stock photos.

These figures were produced between 1985 and 1986 by IGA Plasticos in Mexico (l to r): Gears, Bumblebee (white and blue), Windcharger (yellow, red, and white), Cliffjumper, Huffer, and Brawn. *Courtesy of Ronen Kauffman of toylab.info*

Released as Pipes in Mexico, this toy was actually a Huffer figure in Pipes colors. These are two different versions of the figure. *Courtesy of Ronen Kauffman of toylab.info*

These were manufactured by Lynsa in 1986 for release in Chile and Peru. *Courtesy of Ronen Kauffman of toylab.info*

Created by Estrela, these were the first series of figures released for the Brazilian market. *Courtesy of Ronen Kauffman of toylab.info*

Optimus Volks, a.k.a. Bumblebee. *Courtesy of Ronen Kauffman of toylab.info*

Optimus Carrera, a.k.a. Cliffjumper. *Courtesy of Ronen Kauffman of toylab.info*

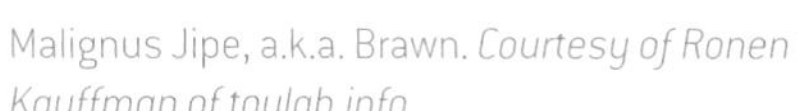

Malignus Jipe, a.k.a. Brawn. *Courtesy of Ronen Kauffman of toylab.info*

Optimus Sedan, a.k.a. Bumper. *Courtesy of Ronen Kauffman of toylab.info*

Malignus Camaro, a.k.a. Windcharger. *Courtesy of Ronen Kauffman of toylab.info*

From l to r: Volks (Optimus), Pick-Up (Malignus), and Carrera (Optimus), a.k.a. Bumblebee, Gears, and Cliffjumper. *Courtesy of Ronen Kauffman of toylab.info*

From l to r: Sedan (Optimus), Camaro (Malignus), and Jipe (Malignus), a.k.a. Bumper, Windcharger, and Brawn. *Courtesy of Ronen Kauffman of toylab.info*

Believed to be from 1986, these were Estrela's second series of Minicars. Estrela created their own factions of heroic Optimus and evil Malignus. *Courtesy of Ronen Kauffman of toylab.info*

In Brazil, Estrela made Bumper an actual character, rather than a mis-carded production error. This is the only known Generation One art for Bumper that ever saw an official release. *Courtesy of Ronen Kauffman of toylab.info*

This Brawn figure was manufactured by El Greco for the Grecian market. *Courtesy of Ronen Kauffman of toylab.info*

A Greek Huffer mis-carded on a Brawn cardback. Variations like these tend to sell for a bit more to collectors of curiosities. *Courtesy of Ronen Kauffman of toylab.info*

Finally, a comparison of the Hasbro Huffer (left) and the El Greco Huffer (right). *Courtesy of Ronen Kauffman of toylab.info*

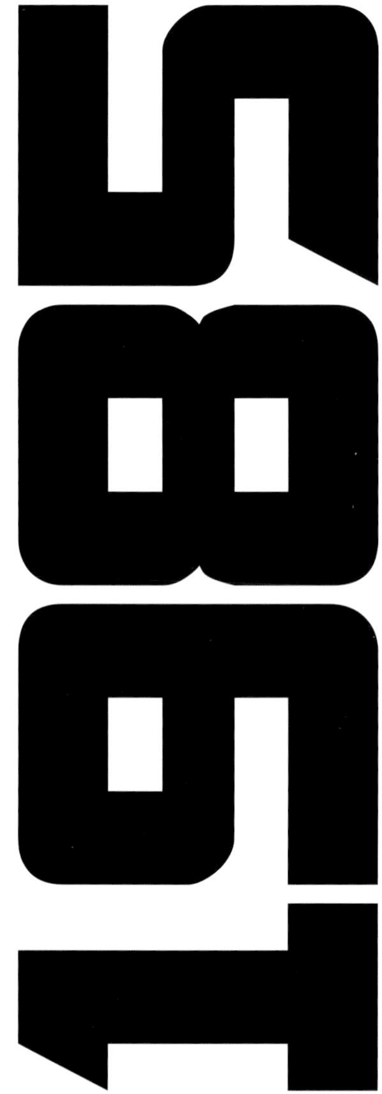

CHAPTER TWO

By 1985, The Transformers were a major success for Hasbro. So much so that Takara abandoned the Diaclone and Micro Change toy lines and began officially selling The Transformers in the Japanese market. In addition to expanding the line, Hasbro re-released the entire 1984 lineup of toys now with "rubsigns." Rubsigns were heat sensitive stickers which revealed the allegiance of a particular toy. With GoBots still in the marketplace, these stickers also served to inform consumers which items in children's collections were official Transformers products. In essence, this was the first long-lasting gimmick introduced into the toy line besides the core concept of transformation. Rubsigns continued to appear on Transformers for the next few years and have even returned intermittently since then. Because rubsigns were a new part of the Transformers brand and not necessarily put into all facets of production at the start of the year, you will find numerous circumstances where figures from 1985 have and do not have rubsigns.

The re-released 1984 Minicars now came with free incentive figures packed right on to the backer card. These transforming figures were called Mini-spies. There were four distinct designs: a Jeep, a Porsche, a Dune Buggy, and a Mazda type sedan. All four versions came in yellow, blue, or white, and were randomly packaged. The Mini-spies also featured a pull-and-go motor that allowed them to roll forward when pulled back.

This year also saw the first release of what fandom has come to refer to as Gestalts, now commonly known as Merge Groups, Combiners, or Combiner Groups. Most Combiner Groups of this era consisted of five characters each with a vehicle mode, a robot mode, and a combined mode to form a larger robot once all five components were assembled together. The first ever Combiner Group consisted of six Constructicons. These toys had previously been part of Takara's Diaclone line, but were released in drastically different colors. Because this was another carry over from Takara's figure library the standard combiner theme was not present (more on that in the next chapter). The limbs had a set way they needed to combine to form the larger robot named Devastator: only Scrapper could form the right leg, only Bonecrusher could form the left arm, and so on. This was not the case for later Combiner Groups.

Additional carry overs from Takara's pre-Transformers Diaclone era toy lines included the Insecticons, the Dinobots, the Triple Changer Blitzwing, both Jumpstarters, and several of the new (standard sized) Autobot cars. The Insecticons were meant to be released as part of the 1984 Transformers toy line but were pushed back until 1985. Perceptor and Blaster came from Micro Change.

In addition to repurposing toys from Takara's early figure archives, Hasbro also licensed the use of several transforming figures from various Takatoku Toys product segments from their new owner, Bandai. At the time Bandai had a very limited presence in the United States and granted Hasbro the license to release these figures under the Transformers moniker. Takara would not be able to release these toys in Japan, being in direct competition with Bandai in the Japanese markets, in addition to consumers' extensive knowledge of Bandai and Takatoku Toys in Japan. Much like many of the early Takara toys, these figures included die-cast metal parts and consisted of Roadbuster, Whirl, Jetfire, and the four Deluxe Insecticons. Except for Jetfire, who was the Takatoku Toy of a Super Valkyrie VF-1S from Robotech, these figures had very little fiction prior to becoming Transformers.

The year 1985 was also the first Hasbro offered mail-away figures. The Omnibots and Powerdashers were available in the same booklet, along with another premium that was not a toy: a wristwatch in the shape of an Autobot symbol named the Time Warrior. When you pressed a button at the bottom of the Autobot symbol it would split in two and the time was digitally displayed on the inside.

The other premiums available this year were special promotional pieces. The first came from Cookie Crisp cereal and was a Jazz figure. A lesser-known premium is the Cracker Jack cereal Jazz. Because the same company made both cereals the figures were identical. Finally Pepsi offered a regular Optimus Prime that came with Pepsi stickers glued on the package. These stickers could then be placed on the trailer for Optimus Prime. The Pepsi promotion was available in the United States and Canada. Canada's version of the stickers were wider and fit better on the trailer, resting within the molded recess where Optimus Prime's outside trailer stickers fit.

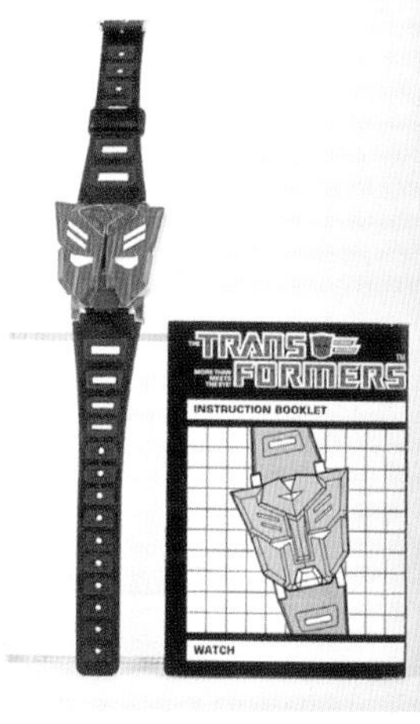

Mail-away Time Warrior watch

1985 CHECKLIST

Autobot Minicars (Carded with Mini-Spies)
* Each figure came with and without Rubsigns.
Bumblebee (yellow body)
Bumblebee (red body)
Cliffjumper (yellow body)
Cliffjumper (red body)
Huffer
Windcharger
Gears
Brawn (Retooled face)

Mini-Spies (both Autobots and Decepticons)
Jeep: blue, yellow, white
Porsche: blue, yellow, white
Dune Buggy: blue, yellow, white
Mazda Sedan: blue, yellow, white

Autobot Minicars (Carded)
* Variations include white and grey borders around the packaging art.
Seaspray
Powerglide
Beachcomber
Cosmos
Warpath

Autobot Jumpstarters (Boxed)
Twin Twist
Topspin

Autobot Cars (Boxed)
Grapple
Hoist
Inferno
Red Alert
Skides
Smokescreen
Tracks

Autobot Dinobots (Boxed)
Grimlock
Slag
Sludge
Snarl
Swoop

Autobots Deluxe Vehicles (Boxed)
Roadbuster
Whirl with cockpit cage
Whirl with plain cage

Autobot Omnibots (Mail Order Boxes)
Camshaft
Downshift
Overdrive

Autobot Powerdashers (Mail Order Boxes)
Powerdasher – Car
Powerdasher – Drill
Powerdasher – Jet

Other Autobots (Boxed)
Blaster
Jetfire
Jetfire with Robotech symbol on wing
Omega Supreme
Perceptor
Pepsi Promo Optimus Prime
Cookie Crisp Promo Jazz
Cracker Jack Promo Jazz

Decepticon Constructicons (Carded)
Bonecrusher
Hook
Long Haul
Mixmaster
Scavenger
Scrapper

Devastator – Constructicon Gift Set (Boxed)

Decepticon Insecticons (Boxed)
Bombshell
Kickback
Shrapnel

Decepticon Deluxe Insecticons (Boxed)
Barrage
Chop Shop
Ransack
Venom

Decepticon Triple Changers (Boxed)
Astrotrain
Blitzwing

Decepticon Jets (Boxed)
Dirge
Ramjet
Thrust

Other Decepticons (Boxed)
Shockwave

Besides the rubsigns, an obvious difference between the 1984 and 1985 Minicars is how they were packaged. All re-release from the 1984 series now came affixed to their card backs transformed into robots. Some Bumblebee card backs came with a red Bumblebee pictured in vehicle mode, while some Cliffjumper card backs came with the image of a yellow Cliffjumper instead of the red. Bumper was not re-released in 1985. *Courtesy of Dan Hodgkinson*

A small adjustment was made with the Brawn figure of this year: instead of being molded from one part, the face now consisted of two separate pieces. Without a rubsign, you can tell the difference by looking at the faceplate. If there are slits on the inside where it meets the silver of the head it is the second and more common version.

Red body Bumblebee with Mini-Spy.
Courtesy of Chuck Liu of artfire2000.com

The Mini-spies came randomly packaged on the later 1984 re-releases. The four types of Mini-spies did not have individual character names and came yellow, blue, and white.

From l to r: Porsche, Jeep, Dune Buggy, and Mazda sedan. Loose Mini-spies can range in price from $15 to $20, but if it was the last version you needed to complete the collection of twenty-four you could pay a lot more. *Courtesy of Orson Christian of CapturedPrey.com*

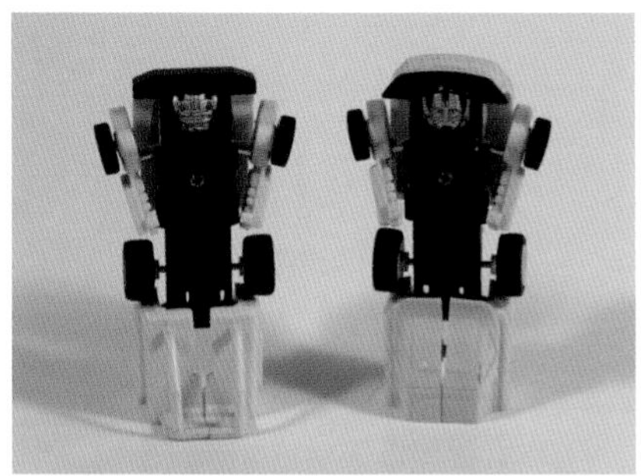

White versions of the Mini-Spies.

All four Mini-spies in all three colors came in Autobot and Decepticon factions; their rubsigns would reveal their allegiance. *Courtesy of Orson Christian of CapturedPrey.com*

Five new Minicars were introduced in 1985. In robot mode (l to r): Beachcomber, Seaspray, Powerglide, Warpath, and Cosmos.

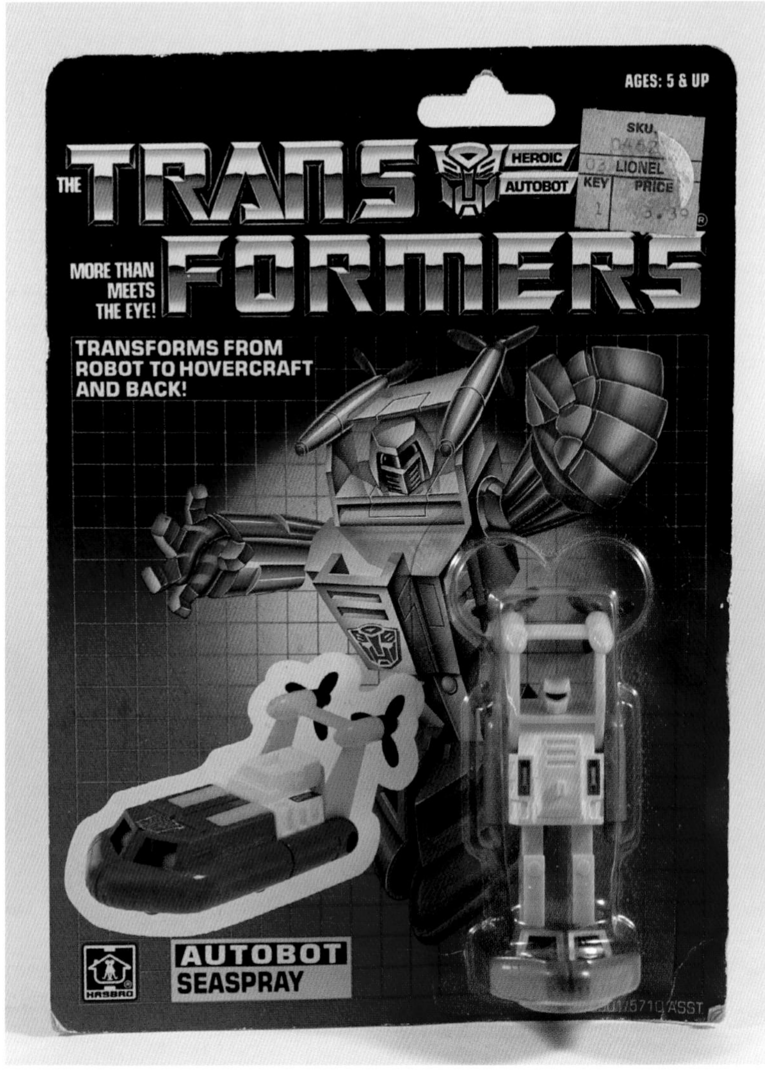

The new Minicars from 1985 were released with a hard-to-find white border and the common gray border. Besides the difference in border colors there do not appear to be differences among the figures.

Greek versions of Seapray and Warpath produced by El Greco. *Courtesy of Ronen Kauffman of toylab.info*

Much like the year before, the Minicars were released individually boxed rather than carded in Japan. *Courtesy of Ronen Kauffman of toylab.info*

At right is a standard Hasbro release Warpath, while on the left is a version which has been dubbed the "bearded" version. The origin of this variant seems to cause confusion among collectors. It appears the injection points on the head match other versions stamped "Takara Japan." It is most likely a non-US variant, but its country of origin remains unknown. *Courtesy of Ronen Kauffman of toylab.info*

The Listen 'N Play audio set came with either a yellow or red Cliffjumper. The story features various characters, but it seemed to be written with little knowledge of established fiction of either the television series or the comic books.

Like the Mini-spies, the Jumpstarters featured a pull back motor. By pulling them backward in vehicle mode and releasing them, the Jumpstarters would roll forward and flip on to their feet.

When printed the Jumpstarters boxes had a mistake on the back of them: the Twin Twist box had the Topspin image and tech-spec (character biography) on the back of it, and the Topspin box had the Twin Twist image tech-spec. A Jumpstarter sealed in the box sells for $85 to $120.

Released in 1985, Salt-Man Z was a South American repaint of Twin Twist. The Spanish and Portuguese word for jump is saltar, so Salt-Man could translate to Jump-Man. Despite being an international variant, Salt-Man Z and the Topspin version named Salt-Man X are not often in demand by collectors. Sealed in the box $40 to $50 would be the maximum these figures would sell for.

Inferno, Tracks, and Grapple. Inferno was previously released in the Diaclone line by Takara. In South Korea, a plagiarized version of this early Inferno co-starred in the animated feature film *Phoenix King*, which was later dubbed and retitled *Defenders of Space*. Tracks was designed by Takara to be a part of Diaclone but was never released, as that line ended in favor of Takara releasing The Transformers in Japan. Grapple was a repaint and slight retool of Inferno. *Courtesy of Orson Christian of CapturedPrey.com*

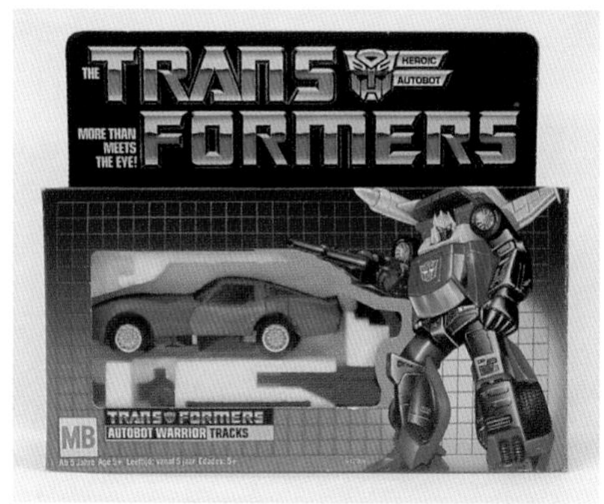

The standard Hasbro version of Tracks in blue. A red version of Tracks was available mostly in the Netherlands, as well as in some other parts of Europe where Milton Bradley Transformers were shipped. This item could range between $3,500 and $5,000. *Courtesy of Chuck Liu of artfire2000.com*

Courtesy of Chuck Liu of artfire2000.com

A sealed 1985 Grapple in the package can sell from $800 to $1,000. *Courtesy of Dan Hodgkinson*

Skids, Red Alert, and Hoist. All three had similarly colored versions released by Takara via Diaclone. Red Alert was a very slight retool of Sideswipe. *Courtesy of Ronen Kauffman of toylab.info*

A side-by-side comparison of a North American (right) and European Hoist both sealed in box. The difference is the suggested age print on the lower left hand side of the boxes. *US Hoist Courtesy of Dan Hodgkinson*

Smokescreen was a slight retool of Prowl/Bluestreak. Sealed in box. *Courtesy of Chuck Liu of artfire2000.com*

Kickback, Shrapnel, and Bombshell. Originally intended to be released in the 1984 line up, they were pushed back until 1985. The Insecticons were originally released by Takara as part of the Diaclone line and named Waruders. The Takara Kickback had much sharper wing tips that the Hasbro version had rounded off due to safety concerns.

The Deluxe Insecticons were licensed by Hasbro from Bandai and designed by Takatoku Toys. They were all first released in a toy line named Armored Insect Battalion Beetras. From l to r: Venom, Ransack, Chop Shop, and Barrage. *Courtesy of Orson Christian of CapturedPrey.com*

As Takatoku Toys went out of business their assets where purchased by Bandai. Having a limited presence in the United States at the time, Bandai licensed these figures to Hasbro. This is why Takara could not release them in Japan. Not only would Takara need to obtain a separate license for their use, but Bandai remains one of Takara's largest competitors in the Japanese marketplace.

Mint and sealed Deluxe Insecticons can sell for $1,200 to $1,500.

As Triple Changers, Blitzwing had a tank and jet mode with spring-loaded missiles. Astrotrain could change into a train or space shuttle.

Triple Changers Astrotrain and Blitzwing. Blitzwing was another carry-over from the Diaclone line in Japan. Astrotrain was also designed by Takara for that line, but did not see release until the Transformers toy line. The Japanese version of Astrotrain is pure white with black wings and train panels.

Takara's version of Astrotrain was white and black to better resemble an actual space shuttle. Due to the reissue of this figure in 2005, the price of this once extremely valuable piece has come down to $350 to $400 if sealed. *Courtesy of Chuck Liu of artfire2000.com*

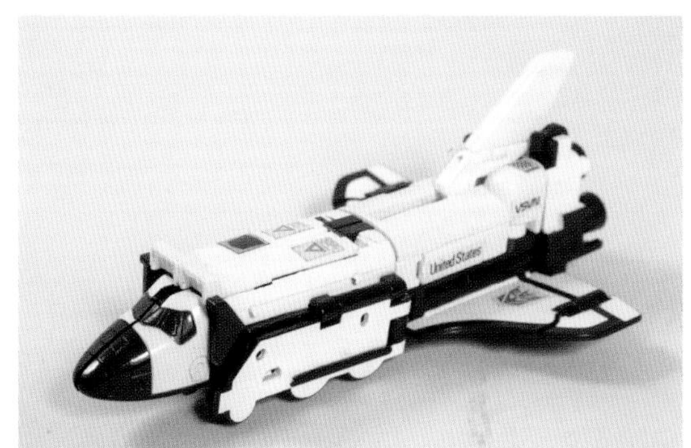

Courtesy of Chuck Liu of artfire2000.com

Thrust, Dirge, and Ramjet were slight retools of the Seeker mold (Starscream, Thundercracker, and Skywarp) from 1984. Each came with unique wings and Dirge and Ramjet sported new weapons. *Courtesy of Orson Christian of CapturedPrey.com*

Dirge. *Courtesy of Donovan Talley*

Ramjet. *Courtesy of Chuck Liu of artfire2000.com*

Bonecrusher, Scavenger, and Mixmaster. These figures were the first Combiners from the Diaclone toy line, and as such the five-member standard Combiner team transformation design did not exist. Unlike other Combiner Groups, each member of the Constructicons formed a dedicated piece of their larger robot. *Courtesy of Orson Christian of CapturedPrey.com*

In robot mode (l to r) are Scrapper, Long Haul, and Hook. The Constructicons were the first Combiner Group released in the Transformers line. *Courtesy of Orson Christian of CapturedPrey.com*

By using additional parts such as forearms, hip connectors, fists, a chest plate, and a head, the Constructicons' combined form resulted in the creation of Devastator. Without these parts Devastator could not be formed. *Courtesy of Orson Christian of CapturedPrey.com*

Hasbro and Takara released the Constructicons individually, but also in Gift Sets. The Hasbro versions came carded and the Takara versions came individually boxed. *Courtesy of Dan Hodgkinson*

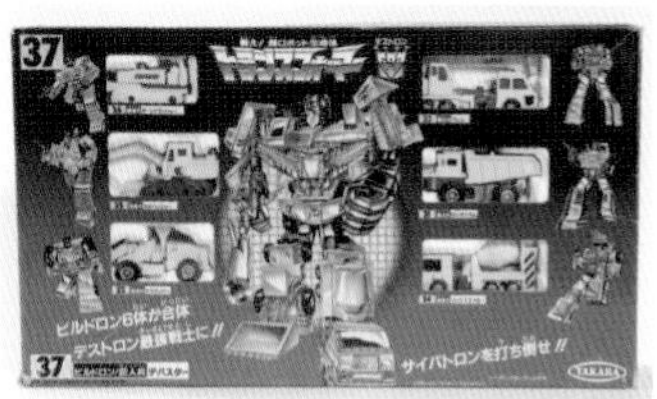

The Takara Constructicon Gift Set. *Courtesy of Chuck Liu of artfire2000.com*

The parts used to create Devastator could also be placed on the Constructicons' vehicle modes, creating an armored look. *Courtesy of Orson Christian of CapturedPrey.com*

Much like the Takara versions, where each Constructicon character came individually boxed rather than carded, GiG also released the Construticons boxed in Italy. *Courtesy of Chuck Liu of artfire2000.com*

Produced in France by toy manufacturer Ceji, the Constructicons were sold in yellow instead of the standard green. These are not to be confused with the Generation 2 versions, which do not have the rubsigns, or the European release from the early 1990s, which did not have the components to form Devastator. *Courtesy of Chuck Liu of artfire2000.com*

Ceji Devastator. *Courtesy of Chuck Liu of artfire2000.com*

Ceji Long Haul and Mixmaster. These carded samples can sell between $250 and $300 each. *Courtesy of Chuck Liu of artfire2000.com*

Dinobots Slag, Grimlock, and Sludge. Being extremely popular and having never been reissued, these figures can sell for $2,500 to $3,500 still sealed. *Courtesy of Dan Hodgkinson*

Previously released in Takara's Diaclone line: Slag, Grimlock, and Sludge. *Courtesy of Orson Christian of CapturedPrey.com*

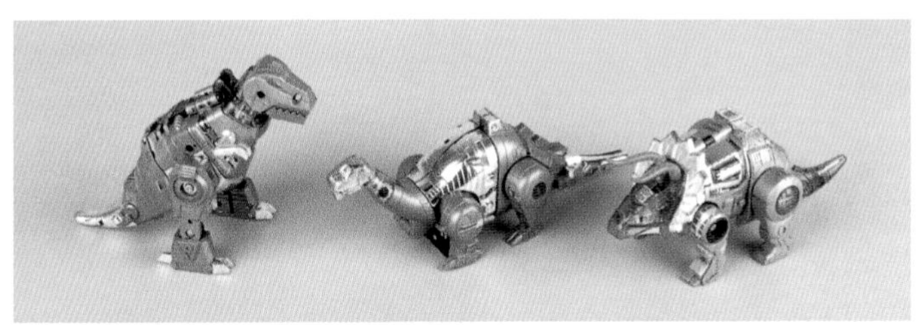

Grimlock, Sludge, and Slag.

The rare Canadian version Slag with a variant red head and missile launcher. *Courtesy of Orson Christian of CapturedPrey.com*

Dinobot Snarl. *Courtesy of Dan Hodgkinson*

Swoop and Snarl. The Diaclone version of Swoop had sharper wing tips, beak, and tail. Like the Insecticon Kickback, these sharp points were remolded to be rounder and not cause potential injury to people. *Courtesy of Orson Christian of CapturedPrey.com*

Dinobot Swoop. Many of the Diaclone figures had cockpits or driver seats for small Diaclone pilots to control the mechs. Swoop is one of the few figures and the only Dinobot who does not feature a cockpit. *Courtesy of Orson Christian of CapturedPrey.com*

Perceptor came with three modes of transformation (robot and microscope are shown).

Perceptor was another carry-over from the Micro Change toy line and was originally named MC-20 Micro Scope.

Perceptor also had what is described as a tank mode. *Courtesy of Ronen Kauffman of toylab.info*

The original Micro Change Blaster had an actual working radio. Residual components of this could still be seen on the Transformers version of the figure.

These two figures were licensed by Hasbro, and neither Roadbuster nor Whirl was released by Takara in Japan. *Courtesy of George Hubert*

Roadbuster was originally designed and produced by Takatoku Toys and released as part of the Starforce under the name Special Armored Battalion Dorvack Mugen Calibur VV-54 AR. Much like the Takara Diaclone toys, the Takatoku Toys Roadbuster and Whirl had seats for similarly sized pilots. Because in the Transformers fiction the characters were sentient robots and not mechs, none of the Takatoku Toys or Diaclone carry-over figures came with pilots. *Courtesy of George Hubert*

During his Takatoku Toys release in Japan, Whirl was named Special Armored Battalion Dorvack Ovelon Gazzette VH-64MR. A variation exists on Whirl's cockpit. Several Whirl figures were released where the cockpit had a cage design painted on the cockpit's plastic. That version is extremely difficult to come by. Seen here is the clear cockpit version. *Courtesy of George Hubert*

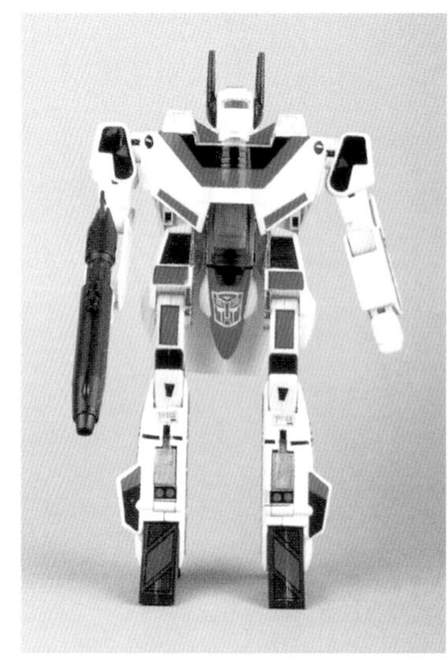

The original Jetfire was released by Takatoku Toys as part of the Super Dimension Fortress Macross toy line based off the Robotech property. Various versions of the pre-Transformers figure were released in Japan in numerous colors, with and without the attachable armor. The VF-1S Battroid Valkyrie version did not come with the attachable armor but the VF-1S Super Valkyrie included the armor.

In Japan there were several tooling and color variations of the armor. The version released with Jetfire was the first type of armor produced. The figure was fully capable of transforming with or without the armor attached.

An extremely rare variation exists of Jetfire with a small circular Robotech symbol stickered on the red stripe of his wing. This would be noticeable with the figure still in the package. Because the Jetfire toy was based off another brand, both the cartoon series and comic books were forced to redesign the character to look inspired by the toy. Takara never released Jetfire in Japan. *Courtesy of Chuck Liu of artfire2000.com*

Shockwave. *Courtesy of Dan Hodgkinson*

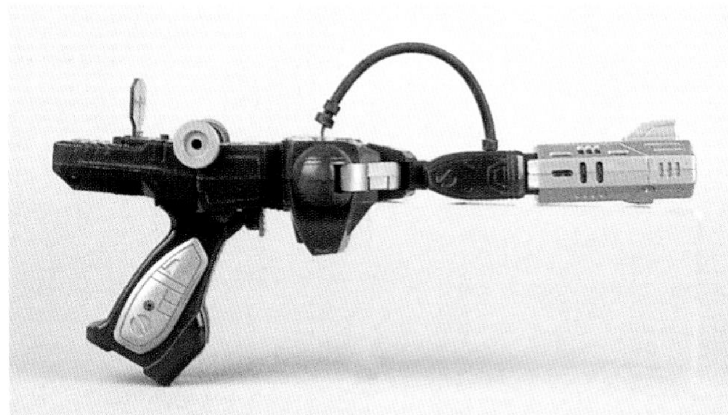

Hasbro and Takara licensed the Shockwave figure for release in the Transformers toy line from Korean-based toy manufacturer ToyCo. The Shockwave figure was previously released in the US and Japan under various names, including Galactic Man, Astromagnum, and Robot Pistol TG-117.

Yet another licensed figure became known as Omega Supreme. Hasbro licensed this from a company called Toybox. This figure was not released in Japan until Takara reissued it in 2008.

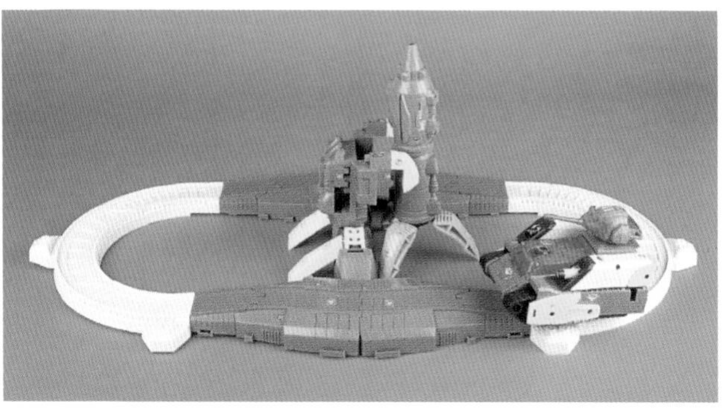

Omega Supreme is not a typical Transformer; he basically needs to be disassembled to form each mode. Battery activated in both modes, while as a robot Omega Supreme has the ability to walk and rotate his light-up head. In vehicle mode the tank will roll around the track. Prior to being part of the Transformers brand, Omega Supreme was released in the US and Japan under the names Omegatron and Mechabot-1.

The three Omnibots were carry-overs from the Diaclone line. Like the other Autobot cars from the Diaclone series, each Omnibot had a driver seat for a small pilot to sit in. Unlike the other Autobot cars they also featured a stealth mode, where some weapons could be deployed while in their car modes. *Courtesy of Orson Christian of CapturedPrey.com*

The Omnibots' Downshift, Overdrive, and Camshaft were mail-away exclusives. The only way to obtain these incentive toys was to purchase a Transformer toy which included a booklet offering these premiums. By mailing in four "robot points" cut from the back of boxes and card backs, along with $5, a random incentive figure would be mailed to you. The more popular of these premiums were the Omnibots. These characters were billed as Autobot reinforcements from Cybertron. *Courtesy of Orson Christian of CapturedPrey.com*

Unlike the Omnibots, the second set of mail-away premiums were not individual characters. These three Diaclone-era carry-overs were simply billed as drill type, car type, and jet type robots. The Powerdashers all had pull back motors that allowed them to roll forward. When the offer was mailed in a random Omnibot and Powerdasher was mailed out. Only the jet type was shown on the booklet. Neither the Powerdashers nor the Omnibots made it in to the television series.

Brawn premiums. *Courtesy of Ronen Kauffman of toylab.info*

The year 1985 also saw McDonalds participate in their first promotional give-away for the Transformers brand. These figures were based on four existing characters and came in six versions each. Because these were only available as test market premiums in the St. Louis area each is extremely valuable. Seen here are all the Bumblebee versions. *Courtesy of Ronen Kauffman of toylab.info*

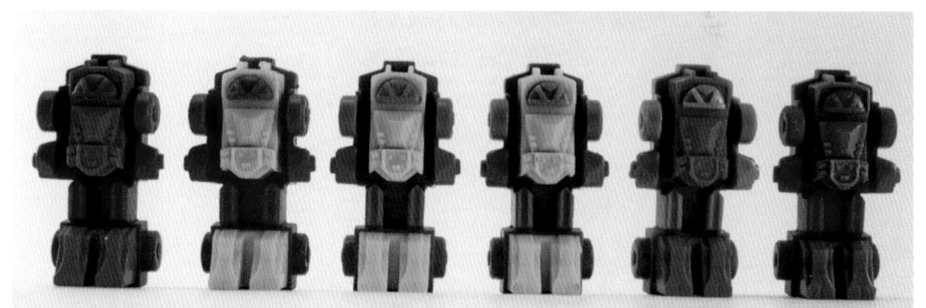

Cliffjumper premiums. *Courtesy of Ronen Kauffman of toylab.info*

Gears premiums. *Courtesy of Ronen Kauffman of toylab.info*

Cracker Jack cereal was only available for about three months, which makes the cereal box and the Jazz premium extremely rare. A Transformers cereal was also in the works which would have had the Jazz mail-away offer, but it never made it on to shelves. This Jazz with the cereal box is worth roughly $5,000+. *Courtesy of Morgan Colyer of iamratchet.com*

The Pepsi Optimus Prime box was a standard off-the-shelf box with the Pepsi information and stickers stickered on the corner. A sealed Pepsi Prime can sell for several thousand dollars. *Courtesy of Chuck Liu of artfire2000.com*

The Optimus Prime Pepsi Promo with affixed Pepsi sticker.

The Canadian version of Pepsi Optimus Prime came with a sticker which covered the whole side of the trailer. *Courtesy of Chuck Liu of artfire2000.com*

Another limited edition Takara Gift Set was the VSY pack with Grimlock, Soundwave, and Frenzy. The Soundwave did not come with the headphones from his previous release and came with Frenzy instead of Rumble. This set also included a comic book and an audiocassette of the comic. A sealed set can range from $3,000 to $5,000. *Courtesy of Chuck Liu of artfire2000.com*

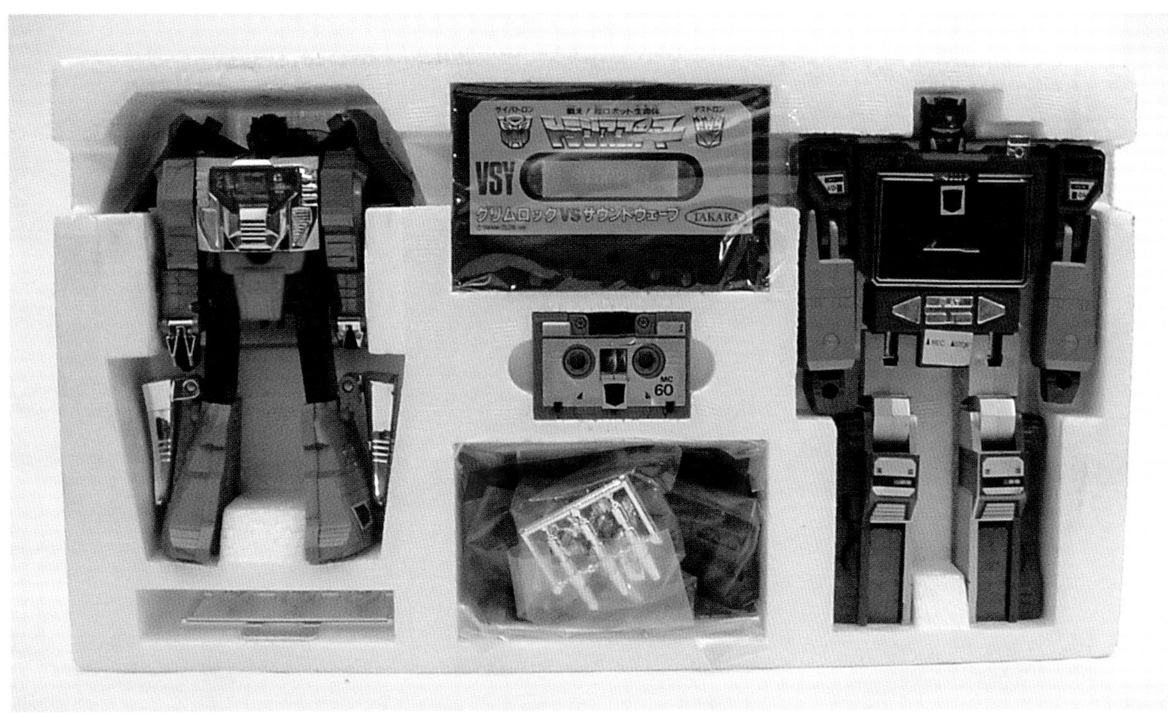

The VSZ set came with Sunstreaker, Skids, and Buzzsaw. *Courtesy of Chuck Liu of artfire2000.com*

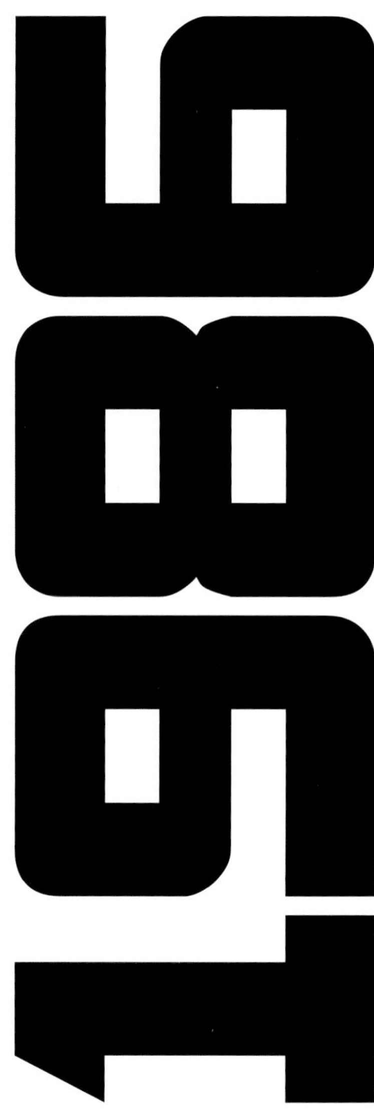

CHAPTER THREE

In 1986, a huge expansion of the Transformers toy line took place. Close to sixty figures would be released this year, along with a theatrical movie based off the ongoing cartoon series. Some re-releases from 1985 would also be included in the line plan, but 1986 signified the beginning of Hasbro and Takara releasing Transformers figures solely designed for the Transformers toy line and not originally produced nor intended by Takara for the Diaclone or Micro Change lines. Despite this there were still some significant carry-overs.

The most important of these carry-overs, and perhaps the most memorable expansions of 1986, were the Combiner Groups. The Autobot Aerialbots and Protectobots, along with the Decepticon Stunticons and Combaticons, shared a unifying design of five combining robots. Each team had a leader who formed the torso and was substantially larger than the four robots who formed the limbs. The limb components were completely interchangeable amongst the group, as each robot had the ability to form either an arm or leg. They were also compatible with any other five robot Combiner Group of the same design type. The ability of interconnected play among the various groups was reminiscent of Takara's Microman toy line. In fact, these combining groups were originally designed and intended by Takara to be part of an offshoot of the Diaclone toy line focused on combination.

The Aerialbots merged to form Superion and could sport a Combaticon leg or a Stunticon arm. The leader robot of each group also had a third transformation mode consisting of a base. The Hasbro versions failed to include the spring-loaded features seen in Takara's Japanese release, which allowed the limb robots to be launched forward when in their vehicle modes. The base (or launch) modes for the Aerialbots leader Silverbolt and the Protectobots leader Hot Spot connected to the giant Autobot city robot Metroplex. Metroplex was also intended by Takara to be part of the combination sub-segment of Diaclone named "Free Combination," but was moved into the Transformers line once Diaclone ceased to be due to the success of the Transformers. Metroplex also sported connecting ports which allowed any of the limb components from any of these new Combiner Groups to plug directly into the side of his arms or on to his shins.

Besides the spring-loaded variations in the combiner group leaders there was another significant variation commonly known to collectors. This is comprised of several combiner group figures being released with metal components and later being offered with plastic ones. The most common area this is found is the chest plates for the Combaticons, Protectobots, and the large combiner group known as the Predicons. As with all other Transformer variants, the metal versions were released first and are the hardest to come by. The change in materials is most likely due to cutting production costs.

Many of the newly designed figures focused around the animated feature film released on August 8, 1986, and the subsequent third season of the television series. Their overall design aesthetic was larger than their Diaclone inspired predecessors. Unlike the 1984 and 1985 Autobot cars, these new figures tended to share a similar scale.

Of noteworthy importance to collectors of in package items are the harder-to-obtain boxes featuring the free poster advertisement printed on the corner. Generally, these box variations are harder to find on the secondary market, particularly for any character from 1985 that was re-released in 1986 with the poster advertisement. Perhaps the most difficult and highly sought after figure is a boxed Blitzwing with the poster ad. These poster variants were only featured on boxed figures. Carded figures, such as the combiner limbs, were redistributed that same year with free reflective patches. The carded figures with the free patch were not as widely distributed as the versions without them.

1986 CHECKLIST

Autobot Minicars (Carded)
* Each figure came with Rubsigns.
Bumblebee (yellow body)
Beachcomber
Cosmos
Powerglide
Seaspray
Warpath

* New for 1986
Hubcap
Outback
Pipes
Swerve
Tailgate
Wheelie

Autobot Aerialbots (Carded)
* With and without reflective patches
Air Raid
Fireflight
Skydive
Slingshot

Autobot Aerialbots (Boxed)
Silverbolt
Superion – Aerialbot Gift Set

Autobot Protectobots (Carded)
* With and without reflective patches
Blades (with metal chest)
Blades (with plastic chest)
First Aid (with metal chest)
First Aid (with plastic chest)
Groove (with metal chest)
Groove (with plastic chest)
Streetwise
* No metal versus plastic variation on Streetwise is known.

Autobot Protectobots (Boxed)
Hot Spot (with metal chest)
Hot Spot (with plastic chest)
Defensor – Protectobot Gift Set

Autobot Cassettes (Carded)
Rewind and Steeljaw (with silver weapons)
Rewind and Steeljaw (with gold weapons)
Eject and Ramhorn (with silver weapons)
Eject and Ramhorn (with gold weapons)

Autobot Triple Changers (Boxed)
Broadside
Sandstorm (with metal toes)
Sandstorm (with plastic toes)
Springer (with metal chest)
Sprinter (with plastic chest)

Autobot Heroes (Boxed)
Rodimus Prime (with metal toes and rubber wheels)
Rodimus Prime (with plastic toes and plastic wheels)
Wreck-Gar

Autobot Cars (Boxed)
* With and without poster advertisements
Hot Rod (with metal toes)
Hot Rod (with plastic toes
Kup (with metal wheels)
Kup (with plastic wheels)
Blurr

Other Autobots (Boxed)
* With and without poster advertisements
Ultra Magnus (with rubber wheels)
Ultra Magnus (with plastic wheels)
Metroplex (with rubber wheels)
Metroplex (with plastic wheels)
Sky Lynx

Decepticon Stunticons (Carded)
* With and without reflective patches
Breakdown
Dead End
Drag Strip
Wildrider

Decepticon Stunticons (Boxed)
Motomaster
Mensasor – Sunticon Gift Set

Decepticon Combaticons (Carded)
Blast Off (with metal chest)
Blast Off (with plastic chest)
Brawl (with metal treads)
Brawl (with plastic treads)
Swindle (with metal chest)
Swindle (with plastic chest)
Vortex (with metal chest)
Vortex (with plastic chest)

Decepticon Combaticons (Boxed)
Onslaught (with metal chest)
Onslaught (with plastic chest)
* No North American version of a Combaticon Gift Set exists.

Decepticon Battle Chargers (Carded)
Runabout
Runamuch

Decepticon Cassettes (Carded)
Ratbat and Frenzy (with gold weapons)
Ratbat and Frenzy (with silver weapons)

Decepticon Triple Changers (Boxed)
Astrotrain (with poster advertisement)
Blitzwing (with poster advertisement)
Octane

Decepticon Jets (Boxed)
* With and without poster advertisements
Cyclonus
Scourge

Decepticon Predicons (Boxed)
Divebomb (with metal chest)
Divebomb (with plastic chest)
Headstrong (with metal chest)
Headstrong (with plastic chest)
Rampage (with metal chest)
Rampage (with plastic chest)
Razorclaw (with metal chest)
Razorclaw (with plastic chest)
Tantrum (with metal chest)
Tantrum (with plastic chest)
* No North American version of a Predicon Gift Set exists.

Other Decepticons (Boxed)
* With and without poster advertisements
Galvatron
Gnaw
Trypticon
Reflector (Mail Order Box)

In 1986, arguably the most important development in the Transformers brand was the introduction of the five team Combiner Groups. These groups featured interchangeable limbs and a dedicated torso robot. All limb and torso Combiner Group figures, whether Autobot or Decepticon, were completely interchangeable. Most Combiner Groups were available in Gift Sets.

The limbs of all teams came carded, while the torso robots came in boxes. This is an example of a Combiner limb with the reflective patch. The limbs were available with and without reflective patches.

In vehicle mode (l to r): Fireflight, Skydive, Silverbolt, Air Raid, and Slingshot. *Courtesy of Orson Christian of CapturedPrey.com*

The development of the Combiners began with the six-member teams of the Constructicons and the Trainbots (released solely in Japan). Takara refined the process by creating a torso bot that also acted as the leader and four limb robots who could transform into either arms or legs. Seen here are the Aerialbots (l to r): Slingshot, Skydive, Silverbolt, Air Raid, and Fireflight. *Courtesy of Orson Christian of CapturedPrey.com*

The combined form of the Aerialbots was named Superion. Collectors typically refer to the animation models of the television series for placement of the limbs.

Silverbolt in base mode with the spring-loaded launcher from Takara. *Courtesy of Chuck Liu of artfire2000.com*

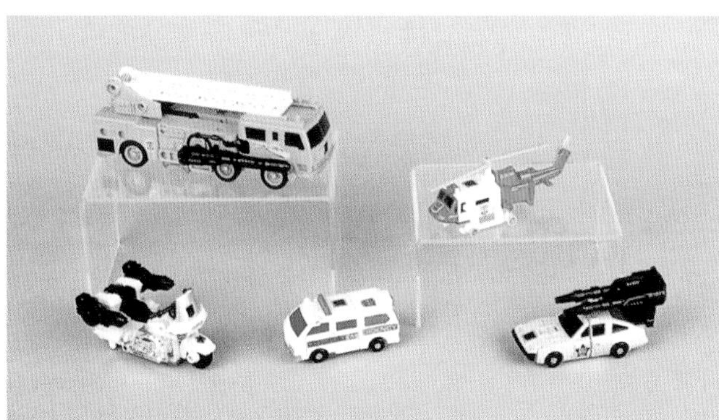

A common variation seen with most Combiner figures of this year are metal versus plastic chests. The die-cast metal chests were the first versions released and are hard to obtain on the secondary market. (For a list of variations please refer to this chapter's checklist.) In robot mode (l to r) are Streetwise, Blades, Hot Spot, Groove, and First Aid. *Courtesy of Orson Christian of CapturedPrey.com*

The combined form of the Protectobots was named Defensor.

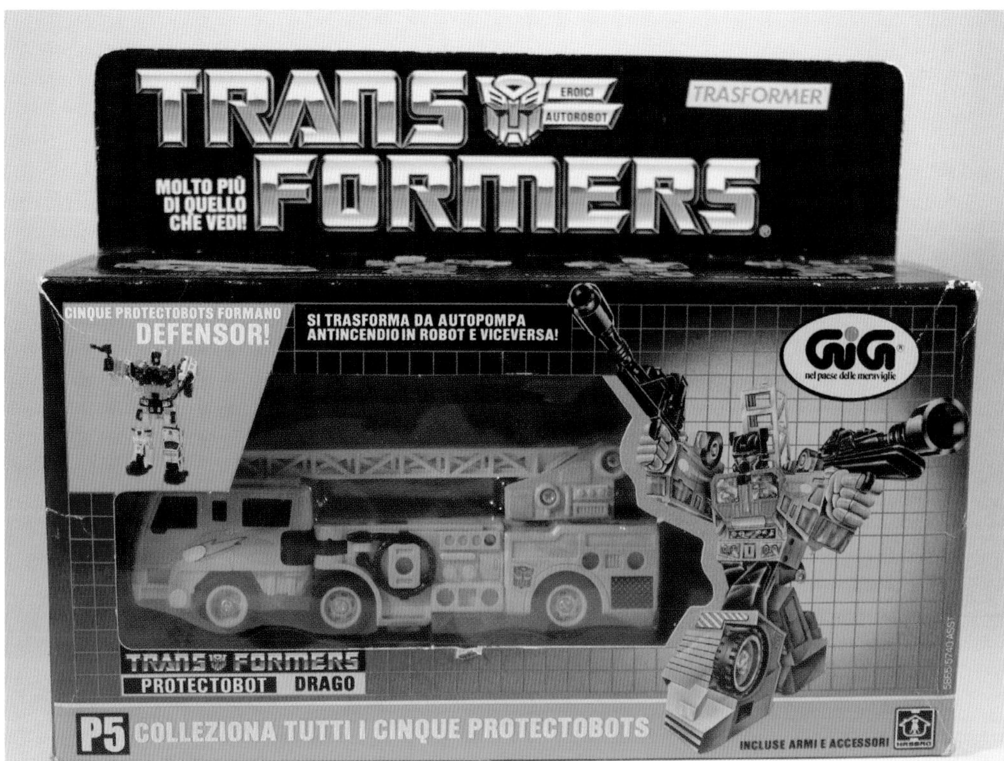

The Italian GiG release of Hot Spot (right) and the Classics reissue (below).

First Aid carded with reflective patch.

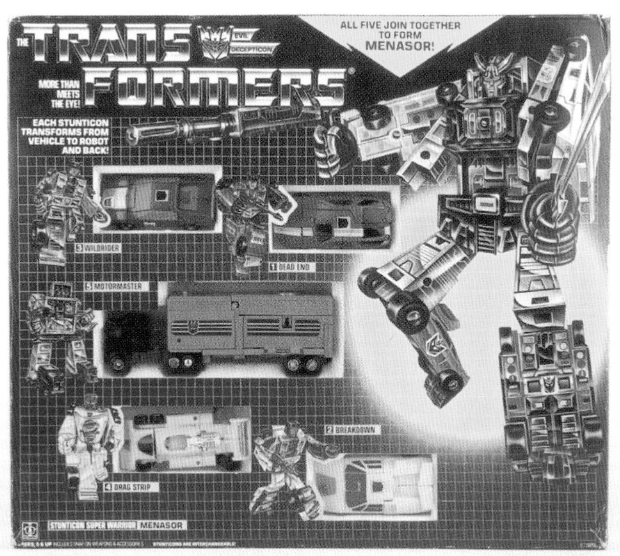

Sealed Gift Sets are extremely difficult to find. A Stunticons Gift Set sealed can sell for $5,000 to $7,000. It is one of the hardest to find US Gift Sets. *Courtesy of Dan Hodgkinson*

Breakdown. *Courtesy of Chuck Liu of artfire2000.com*

The Classics reissue of Drag Strip from the early 1990s.

Drag Strip. *Courtesy of Aaron Archer*

Breakdown, Drag Strip, Motormaster, Dead End, and Wildrider. *Courtesy of Orson Christian of CapturedPrey.com*

Motormaster's base mode and spring-loaded launcher from Takara. *Courtesy of Chuck Liu of artfire2000.com*

Each Combiner Group (except for the Aerialbots) came with additional weaponry which attached to their vehicle modes. These extra components were not able to attach to the figures in any other mode. Extra components for most teams were not interchangeable, the Stunticons being the only exception. *Courtesy of Orson Christian of CapturedPrey.com*

The combined form of the Stunticons was named Menasor.

The Decepticon Combaticons (l to r): Blast Off, Vortex, Onslaught, Brawl, and Swindle. Hasbro never produced a Combaticon Gift Set for the North American markets. Combaticon Gift Sets were available in Japan through Takara and in Italy via GiG. *Courtesy of Orson Christian of CapturedPrey.com*

Seen here is the spring-loaded ramp version from Takara. Alongside it is the base mode where Onslaught could launch most combiner limbs. *Courtesy of Chuck Liu of artfire2000.com*

While Hasbro did not release the Combaticons in a Gift Set in North America, Gig did release them as a set in Italy.

The combined form of the Combaticons was named Bruticus. The Combaticons hold the record for the most repaints of any Combiner Group. It was first repainted and released in 1992, as Battle Gaia during Operation Combination. In 1994, Hasbro released them as part of the Generation 2 line. In 2000, the team was repainted as Baldigus for Car Robots, and later repainted and renamed Ruination for the US version of the Car Robots toy line called Robots in Disguise. Finally, in 2009, Takara produced an Encore reissue in their original colors.

The Classic reissues also failed to come with the spring-loaded launchers of the North American Hasbro releases.

In Japan the Combiner Group limbs did not come carded, rather in boxes.

During the early 1990s, Europe and several other international markets saw the reissue of many Transformers figures. These were often referred to as Classics on the packaging, and all came in what is referred to as gold packaging. Seen here is the Classics Brawl.

The Predacons each came with blasters and swords (l to r): Razorclaw, Divebomb, Tantrum, Rampage, and Headstrong.

A final group of Combiners was released this year that also had metal and plastic chest variants. These larger Combiners were called the Predacons. Despite being a five team Combiner Group, each Predacon formed a dedicated portion of their combined form named Predaking.

Some blasters and Predaking components could connect to the Predacons in their beast modes.

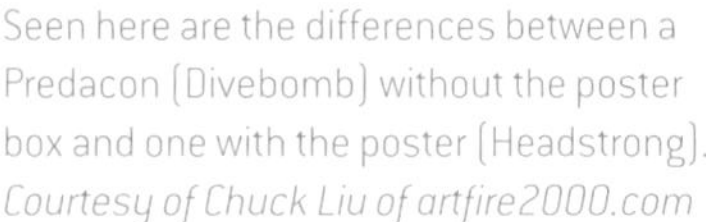

Seen here are the differences between a Predacon (Divebomb) without the poster box and one with the poster (Headstrong). *Courtesy of Chuck Liu of artfire2000.com*

Except for Wheelie, the 1986 Minicars were retools of the original 1984 Mincars. In robot mode (l to r) are Hubcap, Swerve, Wheelie, Outback, Tailgate, and Pipes.

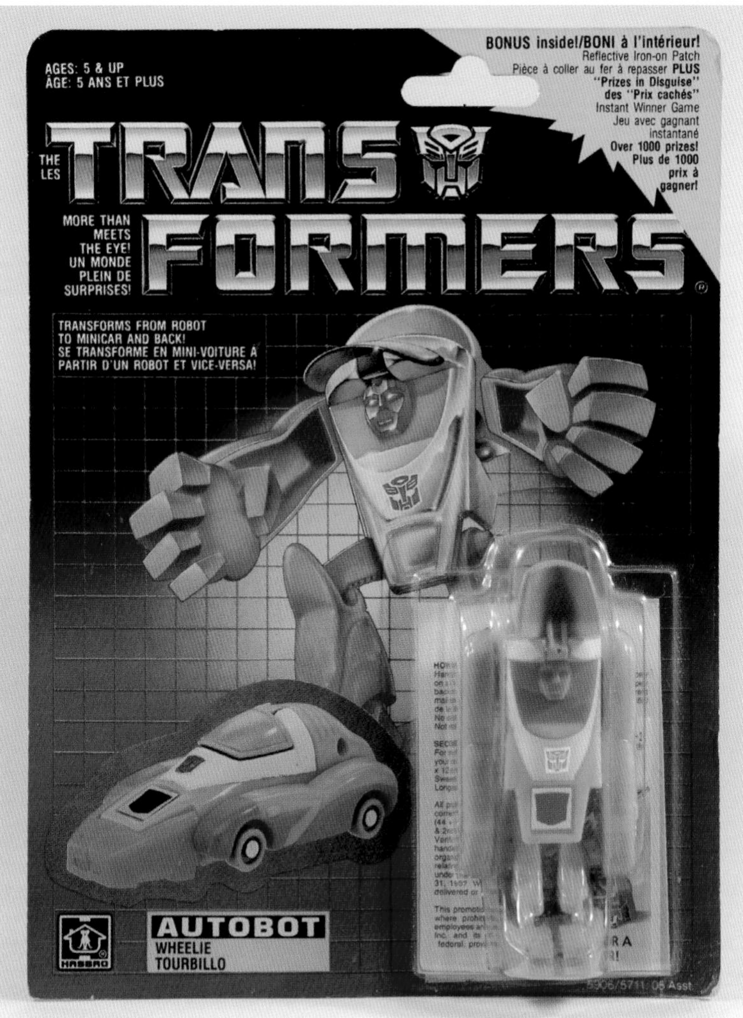

Reflective patches were also available in international markets, as seen here on this European carded Wheelie.

Rewind and Steeljaw with gold weapons. The gold weapons are the more difficult to find.

The year 1986 finally saw the release of transforming cassettes for the Autobot equivalent to Soundwave named Blaster. Available with silver and gold chromed weapons, these tapes came in carded two-packs like their Decepticon counterparts. Here are Eject and Ramhorn with silver weapons.

These cassettes were original designs and not carryovers from the Diaclone line. In cassette form they were the same size as the Decepticon versions and could fit in Soundwave or Blaster's compartments.

In Japan Takara released the 1985 cassettes individually boxed. By 1986, all tapes came carded, including the rereleases of the 1985 cassettes.

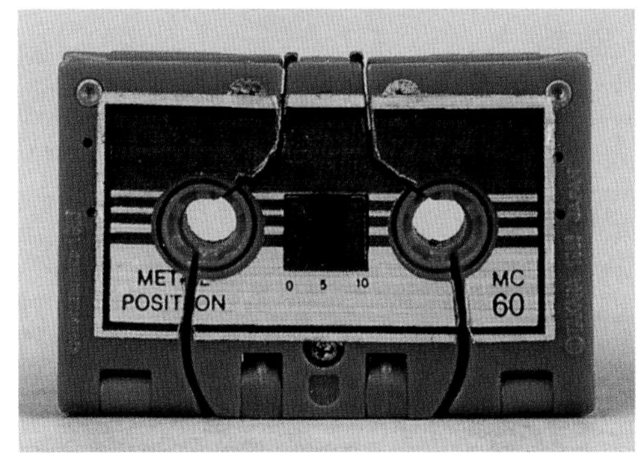

Ratbat was the only new Decepticon cassette released in 1986 and came carded with Frenzy.

Ratbat also had the gold and silver weapons variations. *Courtesy of Ronen Kauffman of toylab.info*

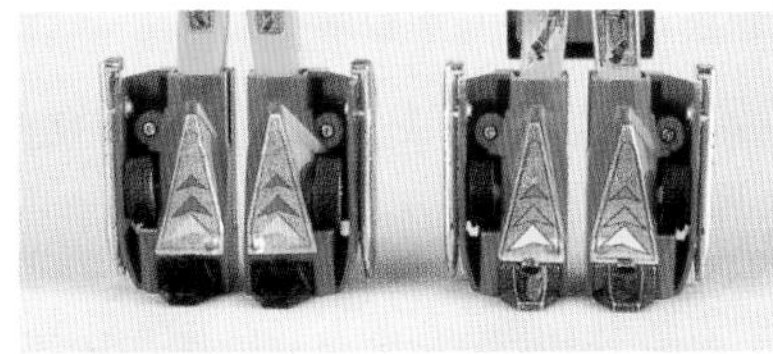

Here you can see the difference between the plastic-toed Hot Rod (left) and the first version released with metal toes (right). Also of note are the sticker variations on the thighs and legs.

The new Autobot cars for 1986 were similar in scale and much larger than the 1984/1985 figures (l to r): Kup, Hot Rod, and Blurr. *Courtesy of Orson Christian of CapturedPrey.com*

After Optimus Prime was discontinued, Rodimus Prime became the new leader of the Autobots. Rubber wheel and plastic wheel variations exist for this figure, as well as slight changes and pigmentation differences in the yellow spoiler. *Courtesy of Orson Christian of CapturedPrey.com*

Wreck-Gar. Unlike many of the other new figures from this year, Wreck-Gar did not have die-cast metal components replaced during later releases. Rodimus Prime and Wreck-Gar were considered Hero size toys at their time of release.

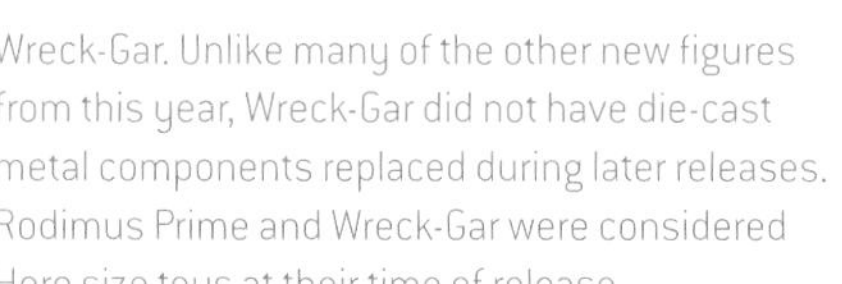

Triple Changers (l to r): Autobots Springer, Broadside, and Sandstorm, and Decepticon Octane. Springer and Sandstorm were initially released with die-cast metal parts. Springer's chest and Sandstorm's feet were later switched to plastic for all later releases.

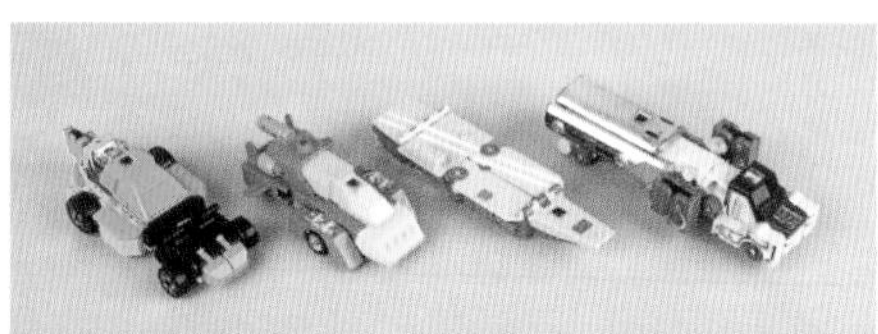

Gnaw the Sharkticon. *Courtesy of Orson Christian of CapturedPrey.com*

The new Decepticon jets this year were Cyclonus and Scourge. Starscream, Dirge, Thrust, and Ramjet were also rereleased in 1986.

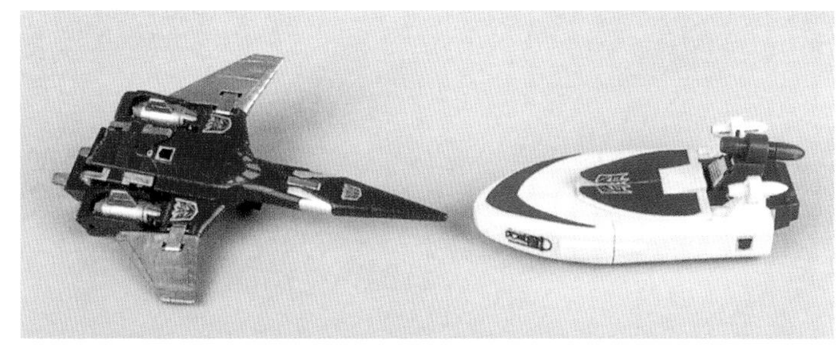

Takara packaged Cyclonus

Most of the boxed figures from this year came with and without the free poster advertisement seen on this boxed sample of Scourge. Typically the poster box variants are harder to find.

Battle Chargers Runamuck and Runabout. *Courtesy of Orson Christian of CapturedPrey.com*

The new leader of the Decepticons was a reformatted Megatron in the form of a new figure named Galvatron. This toy featured lights and sounds, and came with a blaster.

Galvatron sealed can command $550 to $750. *Courtesy of Robert. T. Yee*

Galvatron had three modes: robot, laser cannon, and, by pulling a handle down from underneath his cannon, he could be used as a blaster. A trigger on the handle activated the electronics.

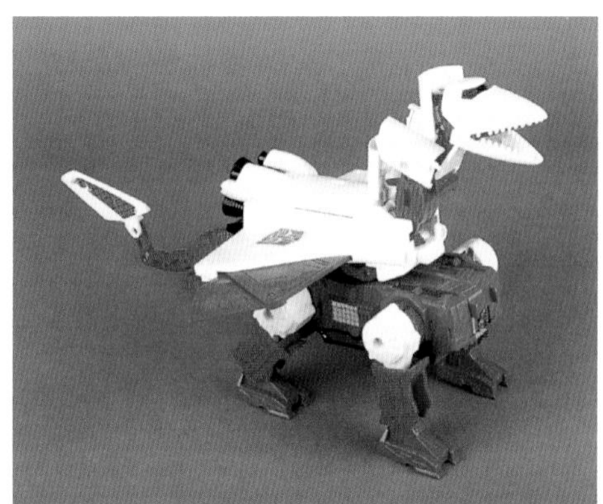

Like Omega Supreme, Sky Lynx was licensed by Hasbro from a company called Toybox for use in the Transformers toy line. Despite being designed by Toybox, Sky Lynx was not previously released. Because Hasbro had gained the license, Takara did not originally release him in Japan until his Encore reissue in 2008.

The battery-powered motor also allowed Sky Lynx to roll forward when in vehicle mode.

Sky Lynx was made up of two robots, but in the fiction they were still the same character. The blue lynx/cargo hold robot featured a battery-powered motor which could allow Sky Lynx to walk in either his lynx mode or his combined mode.

Ultra Magnus boxed with rubber wheels. *Courtesy of Robert T. Yee*

Ultra Magnus boxed with poster advertisement and plastic wheels.

As a transport vehicle Ultra Magnus could carry up to four Autobot cars at a time.

The plastic-wheeled version also came with an unpainted head compared to the more common painted version.

Ultra Magnus was one of the last carryovers from the Diaclone toy line, where he was called Powered Convoy. The Diaclone version came with a small companion transforming robot car who could also seat a pilot. This additional robot has never been released with any version of the Transformers toy. *Courtesy of Orson Christian of CapturedPrey.com*

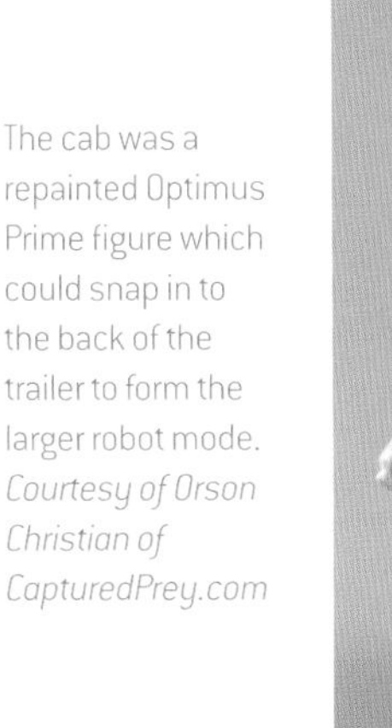

The cab was a repainted Optimus Prime figure which could snap in to the back of the trailer to form the larger robot mode. *Courtesy of Orson Christian of CapturedPrey.com*

Quite a number of minor variations exist on Ultra Magnus, but of significant importance is the rubber-wheeled version, which was eventually replaced with a plastic-wheeled variant. This variation exists on the cab and trailer.

Seen here is the Diaclone version named Powered Convoy. He also came with a smaller robot named Powered Buggy. *Courtesy of Chuck Liu of artfire2000.com*

Metroplex was originally designed as part of the subline of Diaclone toys focusing on combination. Due to that line ending, as Takara switched over to Transformers, Metroplex was released as a Transformer.

This figure could connect any five-team Combiner Group limb to the side of his arms or on to the front of his legs. These features seemed incidental to the Transformers toy line and were never used in any of the fiction. *Courtesy of Orson Christian of CapturedPrey.com*

Courtesy of Donovon Talley

Metroplex came with three smaller robots: Scamper (in black) was able to transform into a car. Six-Gun and Slammer were made from components used to build up Metroplex's robot or city modes.

Metroplex had a launch feature inside his chest for any Minicars or combiner limb that could fit inside. These figures would shoot down the black ramp while in city mode.

Metroplex also had a battle station mode.

The rubber wheels for Metroplex (left) and the plastic wheels (right).

To combat the price point of Metroplex was the Decepticon city base Trypticon. Unlike Metroplex, Trypticon was an original design intended for the Transformers toy line. Trypticon came with a battery-powered motor that allowed him to walk while in robot/dinosaur mode.

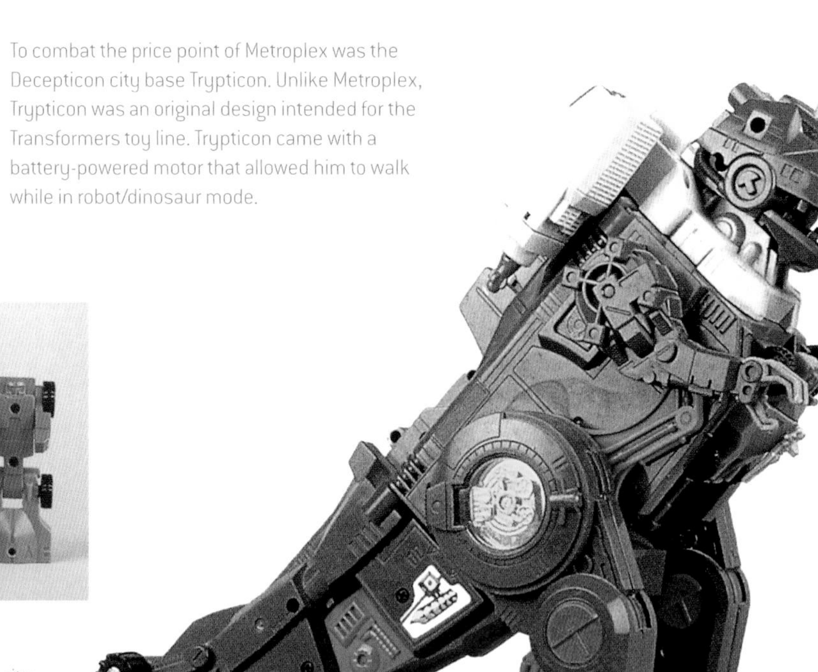

Like Metroplex, Trypticon came with a tank drone (Brunt) comprised of pieces from his city mode and a transforming car named Full-Tilt (right). The cannon on Brunt was electronic and could light up at the flick of a switch.

A sealed Trypticon can sell for between $2,500 and $5,000, depending on the condition of the box. *Courtesy of Chuck Liu of artfire2000.com*

Trypticon also came with a launching mechanism which could shoot Full-Tilt or combiner limbs down his center ramp.

Trypticon in battle station mode.

Beginning in 1986, as the toy line and television show went in new directions, Reflector was finally offered by Hasbro, but exclusively as a mail-away figure, requiring two robot points and $10. From left to right are Spyglass, Viewfinder, and Spectro.

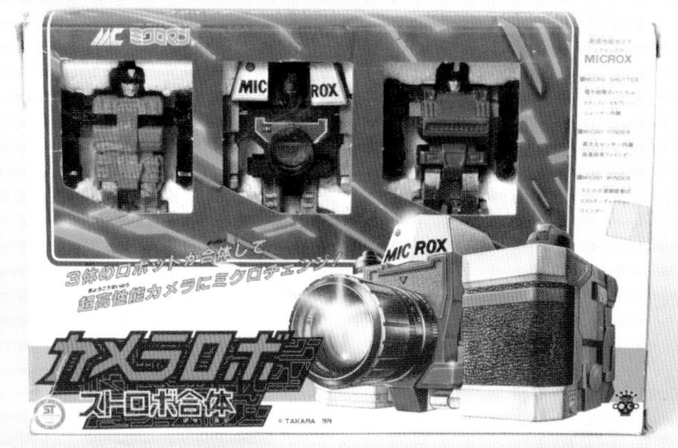

Originally from the Micro Change line, Takara did release Reflector at retail in Japan. *Courtesy of Chuck Liu of artfire2000.com*

Another Takara exclusive was the introduction of Transformers Jrs. These were smaller size figures based on popular characters. Their transformations were similar but simplified.

Transformers Jr. Trypticon. *Courtesy of Chuck Liu of artfire2000.com*

CHAPTER FOUR

As in 1986, some of the previous year's figures would be re-released and new figures were introduced that would continue to lean toward a more space aged design direction. The gimmick that defines this year was definitely the Headmasters.

The Headmaster concept involved a vehicle piloted by a small robot. When the vehicle transformed into robot mode the small pilot robot would then form the head of the larger body. When the head was coupled with the body a display on the robot's chest would show the strength, speed, and intelligence of each character. Each Headmaster pilot was interchangeable with all other Headmaster bodies and would display dedicated strength, speed, and intelligence. This head-swapping gimmick was played up in the Japanese exclusive television series, but not in the US series. If you lost the small robot pilot the larger figure would look incomplete. Takara released six additional and unique Headmaster pilots in Japan as sort of replacements; Hasbro never imported those figures. Additional Headmasters included the Decepticon triple changing Horrorcons, the Decepticon base Scorponok, and the largest Transformer ever released, Fortress Maximus.

An additional key gimmick from this year was the Targetmaster weapons. Similar in size to the Headmaster pilots, the Targetmaster robots transformed into small weapons which could either be held in their larger Transformer companion's hands or attached to their vehicle modes. Unlike the Headmasters, if you lost the Targetmaster weapon you still had the larger robot, which was complete and not missing a head. Like the Headmasters, the Targetmaster robots could be used with any larger Targetmaster companion. Several key characters from 1986 were retooled and released in 1987 as Targetmasters. Variations on these figures include larger holes in their hands and ports retooled into key sections of the bodies that allowed their Targetmaster weapons to attach while in vehicle mode.

Another in-package premium was offered this year in the form of the Decoys. The Decoys were small rubber figures representing characters from the first three years of the line. Their designs seemed to be combinations of their toy and animation models. Autobot Decoys came in red and Decepticon Decoys came in purple, but all the Decepticons Decoys were also released in red. The red Decepticon Decoys are extremely rare. These static figures were only available with carded toys and came randomly packed. Each Decoy was individually numbered on the back.

This year also included several mail-away figures. All were offered in the same brochure and the characters included were Megatron, Thundercracker, Reflector, Optimus Prime, Wheeljack, Sunstreaker, Mirage, Ratchet, Cosmos, Warpath, and the 1986 Hubcap figure named Cliffjumper. A mail-away playset was also offered, including a cardboard playset, a Transformers poster, the techspec manual, membership card, and an iron-on patch. The set was named S.T.A.R.S. (Secret Transformer Autobot Rescue Squad). This promotion was also available in the UK, but the foldout cardboard base was completely different. These sets are extremely difficult to find.

Throttlebot Rollbar seen with the extremely rare Ravage Decoy.

1987 CHECKLIST

Autobot Throttlebots (Carded)
* With and without Decoys
Goldbug
Chase
Freeway
Rollbar
Searchlight
Wideload

Autobot Aerialbots (Carded)
* With Decoys
Air Raid
Fireflight
Skydive
Slingshot

Autobot Aerialbots (Boxed)
* No Decoy
Silverbolt

Autobot Protectobots (Carded)
* With Decoys
Blades
First Aid
Groove
Streetwise

Autobot Protectobots (Boxed)
* No Decoy
Hot Spot

Autobot Technobots (Carded)
* With and without Decoys
Afterburner
Lightspeed
Nosecone
Strafe

Autobot Protectobots (Boxed)
* No Decoys
Scattershot
Computron Gift Set

Autobot Cassettes (Carded)
Rewind and Steeljaw
Ramhorn and Eject

Autobot Headmasters (Boxed)
Brainstorm with Arcana
Chromedome with Stylor
Hardhead with Duros
Highbrow with Gort
Fortress Maximus with Cerebros and Spike

Autobot Targetmasters (Boxed)
Crosshairs with Pinpointer
Pointblank with Peacemaker
Sureshot with Spoilsport
Blurr with Haywire
Hot Rod with Firebolt
Kup with Recoil

Autobot Monsterbots (Boxed)
Doublecross
Grotusque
Repugnus

Autobot Clones (Boxed)
Fastlane and Cloudraker

Autobot Double Spy (Boxed)
Punch-Counterpunch

Other Autobots (Mail Order Box)
Cosmos
Hubcap (labeled as Cliffjumper)
Warpath
Mirage
Optimus Prime
Ratchet
Sunstreaker
Wheeljack

Decepticon Stunticons (Carded)
* With Decoys
Breakdown
Dead End
Drag Strip
Wildrider

Decepticon Stunticons (Boxed)
* No Decoy
Motormaster

Decepticon Combaticons (Carded)
* With Decoys
Blast Off
Brawl
Swindle
Vortex

Decepticon Combaticons (Boxed)
* No Decoy
Onslaught

Decepticon Terrorcons (Carded)
* With and without Decoys
Blot
Cutthroat
Rippersnapper
Sinnertwin

Decepticon Terrorcons (Boxed)
* No Decoy
Hun-Gurrr

Decepticon Duocons (Boxed)
Battletrap
Flywheels

Decepticon Cassettes (Carded)
Ratbat and Frenzy
Slugfest and Overkill

Decepticon Headmasters (Boxed)
Mindwipe with Vorath
Skullcruncher with Grax
Weirdwolf with Monzo
Scorponok with Lord Zarak and Fasttrack

Decepticon Horrorcons (Boxed)
Apeface with Spasma
Snapdragon with Krunk

Decepticon Targetmasters (Boxed)
Misfire with Aimless
Slugslinger with Caliburst
Triggerhappy with Blowpipe
Cyclonus with Nightstick
Scourge with Fracas

Decepticon Clones (Boxed)
Pounce and Wingspan

Other Decepticons (Boxed)
Sixshot
Thundercracker (Mail Order Box)
Megatron (Mail Order Box)
Reflector (Mail Order Box)

Autobot Decoys
1 – Grimlock
2 – Snarl
3 – Swoop
4 – Sludge
5 – Slag
6 – Ratchet
7 – Ironhide
8 – Smokescreen
9 – Grapple
10 – Trailbreaker
11 – Sunstreaker
12 – Skids
13 – Jazz
14 – Inferno
15 – Tracks
16 – Red Alert
17 – Hound
18 – Sideswipe
19 – Prowl
20 – Mirage
21 – Hoist
22 – Wheeljack
23 – Bluestreak
24 – Brawn
25 – Windcharger
26 – Bumblebee
27 – Huffer
28 – Cliffjumper
29 – Blaster
30 – Perceptor
31 – Optimus Prime

Decepticon Decoys
* Both red and purple
32 – Megatron
33 – Skywarp
34 – Thundercracker
35 – Starscream
36 – Soundwave
37 – Bliztwing
38 – Astrotrain
39 – Kickback
40 – Shrapnel
41 – Bombshell
42 – Hook
43 – Scavenger
44 – Bonecrusher
45 – Long Haul
46 – Mixmaster
47 – Scrapper
48 – Devastator
49 – Ravage
50 – Frenzy
51 – Shockwave
52 – Reflector
53 – Laserbeak

The Autobot Headmasters Brainstorm (with Arcana), Chromedome (with Stylor), Hardhead (with Duros), and Highbrow (with Gort). The 1987 Headmasters are typically referred to as Large Headmasters, as 1988 saw the release of the smaller Headmaster figures that are not compatible with their 1987 counterparts. *Courtesy of Orson Christian of CapturedPrey.com*

Highbrow, Hardhead, and Chromedome. *Courtesy of Orson Christian of CapturedPrey.com*

Each Headmaster pilot could fit inside any Large Headmaster vehicle or beast. The heads were also interchangeable with any Large Headmaster body.

Courtesy of Chuck Liu of artfire2000.com

Takara Chromedome.

Headmaster and Targetmaster robots were visible in the package. In a mint in sealed box, a Brainstorm like this could sell for $600 to $900.

Of the Decepticon Headmasters, Weirdwolf is the hardest to find sealed in package. Be aware, there are many knockoffs of various Generation One Transformers; these can appear almost identical to their official counterparts. Vendors often refer to them as reissues. These knockoffs tend to sell from $40 to $60, and are often shipped straight from China. This is Mindwipe, $450 to $550.

Skullcruncher, $450 to $550

Skullcruncher (with Grax), Mindwipe (with Vorath), and Weirdwolf (with Monzo). *Courtesy of Orson Christian of CapturedPrey.com*

The Decepticon triple changing Horrorcon Apeface. Even items not in mint packaging will still sell higher than loose figures. A sealed and mint Apeface can sell for upwards of $800. In a package (right) this item can sell for $200. Except for rare figures—with a package like the one here or in a box with no insert—a collector is basically paying the price of the figure with a slight mark up. *Courtesy of Chuck Liu of artfire2000.com*

Each Large Headmaster has a flip down panel which displays their speed, strength, and intelligence. These meter readings were unique to each head. By swapping a head with another figure, that figure would in turn have that Headmaster head's readouts.

The Horrorcons Apeface (with Spasma) and Snapdragon (with Krunk) had slightly larger bodies than the other Headmasters, yet their heads could still be swapped with other figures.

The Horrorcons were triple changing Headmasters. Both had a beast mode and a futuristic jet mode.

Apeface jet mode and Snapdragon jet mode. *Courtesy of Chuck Liu of artfire2000.com*

Lord Zarak and Fasttrack. *Courtesy of Orson Christian of CapturedPrey.com*

Each of these larger figures had a base or city mode that allowed smaller figures to interact with control panels, repair bays, landing zones, or ramps. Scorponok had a launch mechanism to shoot figures down his center ramp.

Scorponok was the largest Decepticon released for many years. His Headmaster pilot was Lord Zarak. Because Lord Zarak was the standard size of the other Headmasters, the flip down helmet would help his head look more proportional to his body.

By pushing Scorponok forward in beast mode, the rotating wheels would activate his green scorpion legs, moving them up and down.

Courtesy of Chuck Liu of artfire2000.com

In 1987, Fortress Maximus originally sold for $100. Today, a sealed version can sell upwards of $10,000. This price has come down substantially with the Takara Encore reissue in 2013.

Fortress Maximus was the largest Transformer figure released, standing almost two feet tall. In 2015, that title was overtaken by a new version of Metroplex for the Transformers Generations sub line. For scale he is shown with Cog and Spike, two smaller robots that came with him.

The Japanese version came with all new box art. *Courtesy of Chuck Liu of artfire2000.com*

The Japanese version with Master Sword. *Courtesy of Chuck Liu of artfire2000.com*

The third transformation mode was a battle station (or starship with the Japanese version). The dark green cockpit at the top of the tower could seat any Headmaster robot. In Japan, Fortress Maximus came with a large red sword and a small sword for Cerebros.

Cog and Cerebros (with Headmaster Spike attached). Fortress Maximus was a double Headmaster. The standard-sized Headmaster figure Spike would connect to Cerebros (who featured the flip down tech spec panel). Cerebros would then transform and become the head of the larger Fortress Maximus body. Cog was made up of two smaller vehicles named Grommet (blue legs) and Gasket (grey torso).

Without Spike attached, Cerebros would transform into a section of the city mode (right of the center ramp). The city mode featured a detention cell, landing platform, launch ramps, and a small elevator. Gasket and Grommet are in their vehicle forms.

Since losing the Headmaster figure was a problem, Takara sold individually packed alternate Headmaster figures. The first three had robot modes. In robot mode (l to r) are Rodney, Kirk, and Loafer. The second three (l to r) had beast modes: Shuffler, Toraizer, and Lione. *Courtesy of Chuck Liu of artfire2000.com*

Top: Rodney, Kirk, and Loafer. Bottom: Shuffler, Lione, and Toraizer. *Courtesy of Chuck Liu of artfire2000.com*

(l to r): Pointblank (with Peacemaker), Sureshot (with Spoilsport), and Crosshairs (with Pinpointer). *Courtesy of Orson Christian of CapturedPrey.com*

Courtesy of George Hubert

Unlike the Headmasters, the Targetmasters did not have cockpits for their small robot partners to fit in. Instead, the Targetmaster weapons could plug into ports on the vehicle modes. The vehicle ports and fists on each Large Targetmaster body were a standard size and could swap weapons.

Courtesy of Robert T. Yee

Targetmasters Hot Rod (with Firebolt), Blurr (with Haywire), and Kup (with Recoil). *Courtesy of Ronen Kauffman of toylab.info*

Targetmaster Hot Rod sealed, $3,500 to $4,000. *Courtesy of Chuck Liu of artfire2000.com*

Targetmasters Hot Rod, Kup, and Blurr. *Courtesy of Ronen Kauffman of toylab.info*

Targetmaster Kup sells for less, around $1,100 to $1,500. *Courtesy of Chuck Liu of artfire2000.com*

The Hasbro versus Takara packaging for the Targetmasters—Misfire. *Courtesy of Dan Hodgkinson* Slugslinger *Courtesy of George Hubert*

Slugslinger (with Caliburst), Misfire (with Aimless), and Triggerhappy (with Blowpipe).

Targetmaster Scourge is the hardest Targetmaster to find, as he was packed one to every other box. In mint and sealed condition they can sell for upwards of $4,500 to $6,500. *Courtesy of Dan Hodgkinson*

Cyclonus will sell between $2,000 and $2,500. *Courtesy of Chuck Liu of artfire2000.com*

Targetmasters Cyclonus (with Nightstick) and Scourge (with Fracas). *Courtesy of Ronen Kauffman of toylab.info*

Exclusive to Japan were Artfire and Ricochet. These were Targetmasters retooled and repainted from Inferno and Jazz. *Courtesy of Chuck Liu of artfire2000.com*

In 1987, there were two new merge groups: the first was a Decepticon set of Terrorcons. These figures were designed using the same combination method as the 1986 Combiner Groups. The limbs were compatible with those earlier combiner torsos and Metroplex. *Courtesy of Orson Christian of CapturedPrey.com*

The combined form of the Terrorcons was named Abominus.

From right to left are Cutthroat, Sinnertwin, Hun-Gurrr, Blot, and Rippersnapper. *Courtesy of Orson Christian of CapturedPrey.com*

The Terrorcons were never available in North America in a gift set. There is an Italian gift set from GiG and a Japanese gift set (shown) from Takara.

The Technobots were released by Hasbro in a gift set and individually. In a sealed and mint box, the Technobots Gift Set can sell from $7,500 all the way up to $10,500+.

The Technobots were the last Autobot Combiners released by Hasbro in the 1980s (l to r): Scattershot, Nosecone, Afterburner, Strafe, and Lightspeed.

Scattershot (top) and (l to r) Lightspeed, Strafe, Nosecone, and Afterburner.

Like many of the previous Combiner Group leaders, Scattershot featured a supplementary mode. Scattershot was also able to transform into a cannon. *Courtesy of Orson Christian of CapturedPrey.com*

The combined form of the Technobots was named Computron.

The Throttlebots came carded with and without Decoys. Here are Freeway, Goldbug, and Chase. *Courtesy of Robert T. Yee*

Throttlebots Rollbar, Wideload, and Goldbug (formerly Bumblebee). *Courtesy of Orson Christian of CapturedPrey.com*

Throttlebots Searchlight and Freeway.

Seen here for comparison is the UK Classics version of Goldbug. In the fiction this character was a reformatted/rebuilt version of Bumblebee.

Courtesy of Chuck Liu of artfire2000.com

Duocons Flywheels and Battletrap.

The Duocons were two vehicles which could unite and form one robot body. The vehicles were not interchangeable. On the left are the two Battletrap vehicles, and on the right the two Flywheels components.

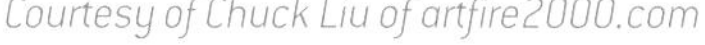

Courtesy of Chuck Liu of artfire2000.com

The clones (or twins) looked exactly alike in robot mode, save for a few parts on their backs. Each robot would turn into different vehicles or beasts. The Decepticon clones were Pounce (a puma) and his clone Wingspan (an eagle). The Autobot clones were Fastlane (race car) and Cloudraker (a jet). Each clone came with two rubsigns: one to designate their allegiance and the other to designate their alternate mode.

Courtesy of Chuck Liu of artfire2000.com

The only Double Spy character ever produced was an Autobot named Punch. Although he had only one vehicle mode, he could transform into two distinct robot modes: Punch and his Decepticon version, Counterpunch. Each robot mode had a rubsign insignia for the appropriate faction. *Courtesy of Orson Christian of CapturedPrey.com*

Punch-Counterpunch came packaged as an Autobot and featured his Autobot and Decepticon artwork on the front of the box. *Courtesy of Chuck Liu of artfire2000.com*

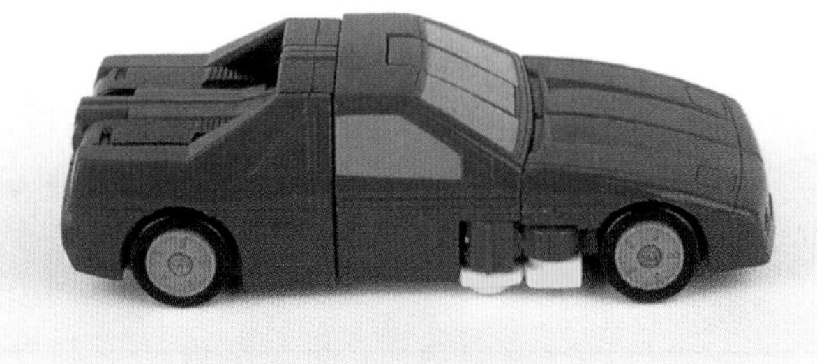

The vehicle mode for Punch and Counterpunch.

Slugest and Overkill. *Courtesy of Orson Christian of CapturedPrey.com*

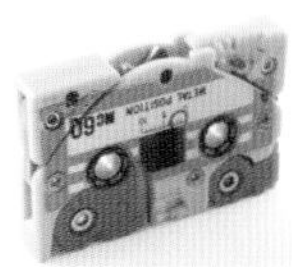

Repugnus, Doublecross, and Grotusque.

The Autobot Monsterbots Repugnus, Doublecross, and Grotusque. *Courtesy of Orson Christian of CapturedPrey.com*

Each Monsterbot transformed into a hideous, monstrous creature. In these alternate forms, each had a trigger that could allow them to shoot sparks from their mouth. Doublecross shot the sparks from his chest.

A first for the Transformers line was the versatile Decepticon Sixshot. This figure had six different modes: a robot . . .

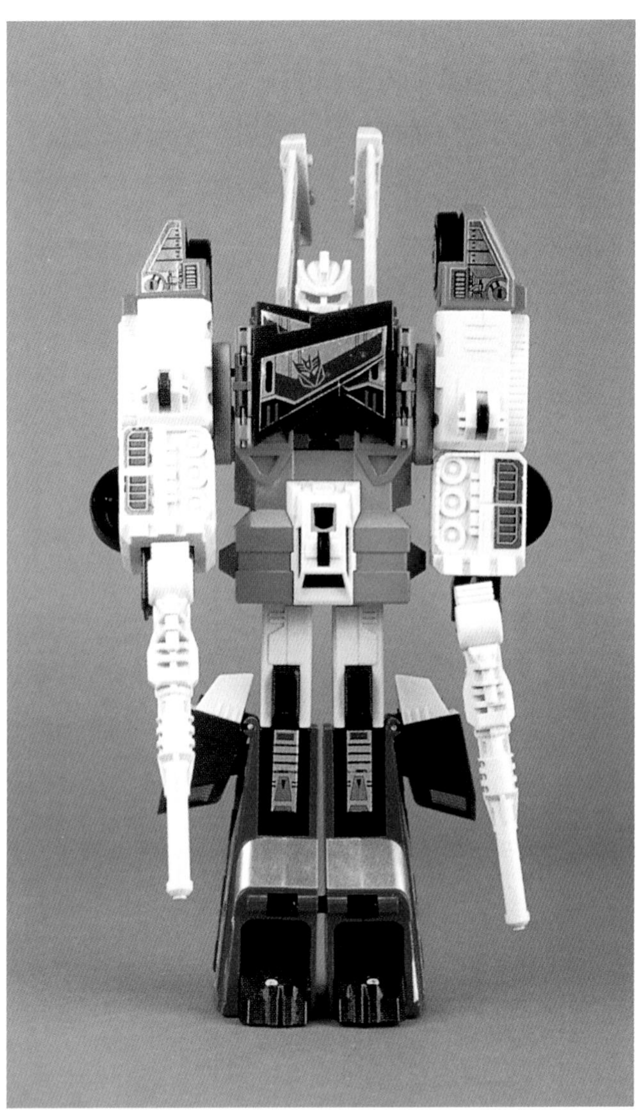

. . . a car . . .

. . . a jet . . .

. . . a tank . . .

. . . a wolf . . .

. . . and finally a blaster (or upside down submarine). Sixshot was not released in the UK. Takara would eventually reissue him several times beginning in 2002.

In 1987, Takara would begin developing exclusive product for their Transformers line. Some of the first figures include Graphy (left) and Noise (right). These Japanese exclusive cassettes are extremely rare to find either loose or in the package. Sealed in the box they can sell for $4,000 to $5,000+ a piece. *Courtesy of Orson Christian of CapturedPrey.com*

Besides having their own animal-based robot modes, Graphy and Noise could merge into a larger robot named Decibel. *Courtesy of Orson Christian of CapturedPrey.com*

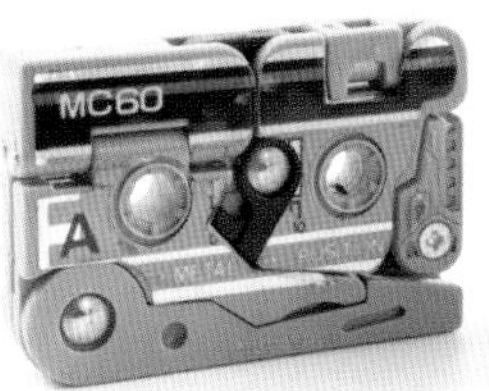

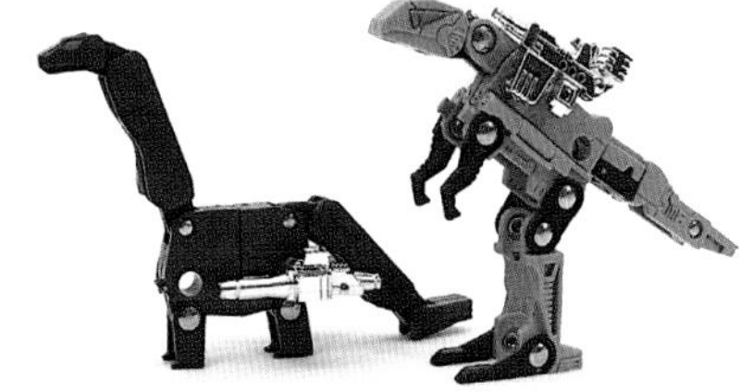

Saur (left) and Dile (right) seem to be even more difficult to find on the secondary market than Graphy and Noise. Their combined form is named Legout. *Courtesy of Chuck Liu of artfire2000.com*

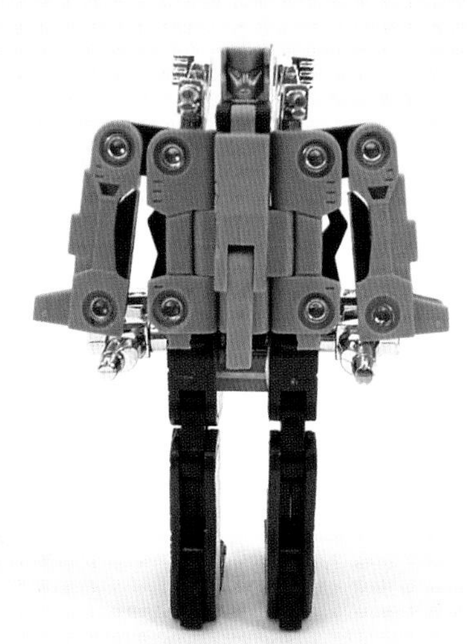

Sealed in the box they can sell for $4,000 to $5,000+ a piece. *Courtesy of Chuck Liu of artfire2000.com*

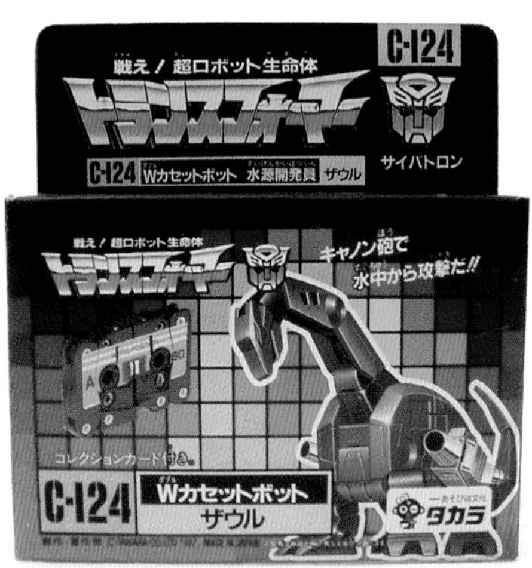

Here is Twincast. *Courtesy of Chuck Liu of artfire2000.com*

In 1987, Takara remolded the Soundwave and Blaster figures to hold two cassettes in their chests. These were the same characters reborn and renamed. Seen here is Soundblaster. *Courtesy of Chuck Liu of artfire2000.com*

Each member of Raiden was released individually, as well as in a gift set. *Courtesy of Chuck Liu of artfire2000.com*

From left to right are Kaen, Seizan, Suiken, Yukikaze, Getsuei, and Shouki. *Courtesy of Chuck Liu of artfire2000.com*

Raiden was another Diaclone-era carry forward and was originally released alongside the precursor to Devastator. Because of this Raiden is a six-member Combiner Group. *Courtesy of Chuck Liu of artfire2000.com*

Each Trainbot was based off a different locomotive. They could also connect together and form one long train. *Courtesy of Chuck Liu of artfire2000.com*

Another Transformers Jr. set was Raiden. Each figure that made up the Raiden Jr. set was sold individually, but was also available in a rare gift set. Sealed this gift set can sell for $3,000 to $5,000.

CHAPTER FIVE

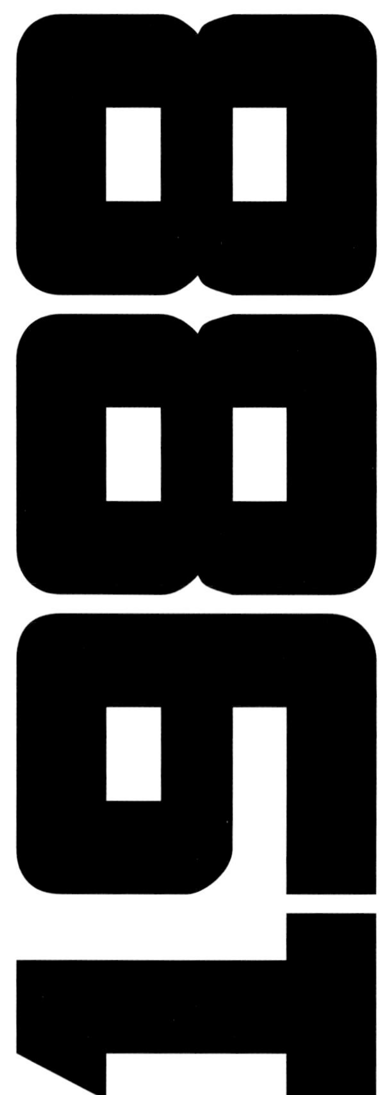

By this year unintentional variants began to drastically slow down, while in Japan Takara was repainting and retooling more and more figures into new characters. in 1988, the most important development was the introduction of the Powermasters and Pretenders.

The Powermasters had small robot companions who transformed into engines. By plugging these engines into their vehicle modes joints on the larger robot would unlock, allowing it to transform into a robot. Most Powermasters came with one companion robot, which were interchangeable with all other Powermaster bodies. Takara also released most of the toys released by Hasbro, but Takara's versions came in different colors and were different characters all together. Takara also created a Double Powermaster with two engines named Overlord. A fairly large figure, Overlord was released by Hasbro in Europe and Australia.

The second main gimmick of this year revolved around the Pretenders. These were large shells with articulation only present in the arms. These shells hid a thin transforming robot within. The inner robots need to use weapons and parts that fit on the shells to complete their transformation into vehicles. Without these extra parts their vehicle forms would seem extremely lacking. The Autobot Pretenders disguised themselves as humans, while the Decepticon shells appeared to be monsters.

Powermaster Optimus Prime was the largest Powermaster released in North America.

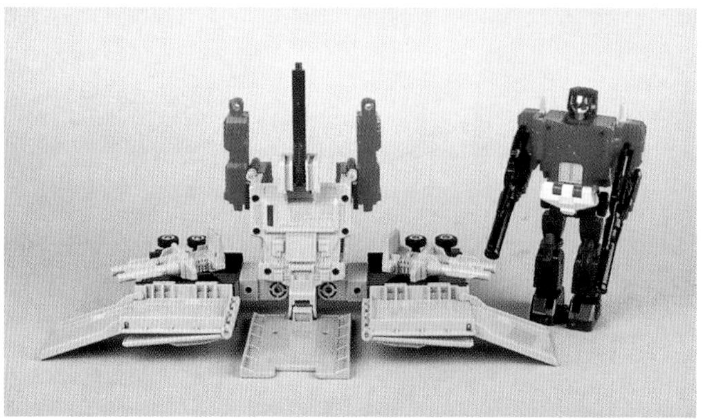

The cab section could transform into its own robot, while the trailer transformed into a base. Powermaster engines could plug in to the grey double cannons.

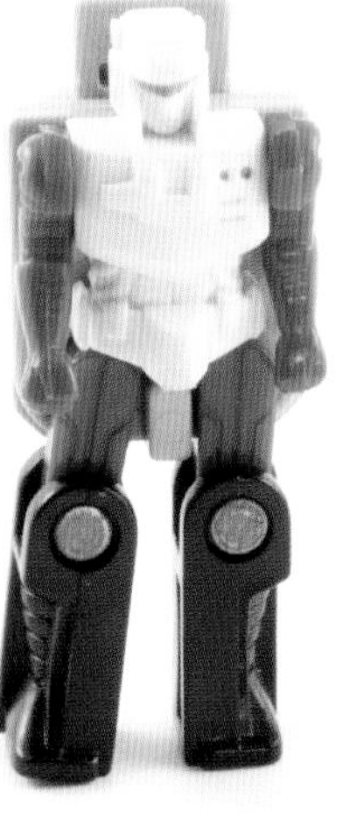

The Powermaster engine for Optimus Prime named HiQ. *Courtesy of Morgan Colyer of iamratchet.com*

1988 CHECKLIST

Autobot Sparkabots (Carded)
Fizzle
Guzzle
Sizzle

Autobot Triggerbots (Carded)
Backstreet
Dogfight
Override

Autobot Cassettes (Carded)
Rewind and Steeljaw
Ramhorn and Eject
Grand Slam and Raindance

Autobot Small Targetmasters (Carded)
Landfill with Flintlock and Silencer
Quickmix with Boomer and Ricochet
Scoop with Tracer and Holepunch

Autobot Small Headmasters (Boxed)
Hosehead with Lug
Nightbeat with Muzzle
Siren with Quig

Autobot Powermasters (Boxed)
Getaway with Rev
Joyride with Hotwire
Slapdash with Lube
Optimus Prime with HiQ

Autobot Pretenders (Boxed)
Cloudburst
Landmine
Waverider
Groundbreaker
Sky High
Splashdown

Autobot Pretender Beasts (Boxed)
Chainclaw
Catilla

Autobot Pretender Vehicle (Boxed)
Gunrunner

Other Autobots (Boxed)
Quickswitch

Decepticon Firecons (Carded)
Cindersaur
Flamefeather
Sparkstalker

Decepticon Seacons (Carded)
Nautilator
Overbite
Seawing
Skalor
Tentakil

Decepticon Seacons (Boxed)
Snaptrap
Piranacon Gift Set

Decepticon Small Targetmasters (Carded)
Needlenose with Sunbeam and Zigzag
Quake with Tiptop and Heater
Spinster with Singe and Hairsplitter

Decepticon Small Headmasters (Boxed)
Fangry with Brisko
Horri-Bull with Kreb
Squeezeplay with Lokos

Decepticon Powermasters (Boxed)
Darkwing with Throttle
Dreadwind with Hi-Test

Decepticon Pretenders (Boxed)
Bomb-Burst
Skullgrin
Submarauder
Bugly
Finback
Iguanus

Decepticon Pretender Beasts (Boxed)
Carniva
Snarler

Decepticon Pretender Vehicle (Boxed)
Roadgrabber

Other Decepticons (Boxed)
Doubledealer with Knok and Skar

The cab could merge with the trailer to form a larger Optimus Prime. *Courtesy of Morgan Colyer of iamratchet.com*

The trailer extension was named Godbomber and was exclusive to Japan. The figure was a Transformer similar to Omega Supreme: it did not really transform, but assembled into a robot. *Courtesy of Orson Christian of CapturedPrey.com*

In Japan, Powermaster Optimus Prime was a completely different character named Ginrai. Ginrai was a human who wore the HiQ armor. When called into battle, he would activate his Transtector (or his mech), which in this case looked like Optimus Prime, and when the cab combined with the trailer his name became Super Ginrai. The toy had darker greys, remolded arms, and die-cast parts the Hasbro version did not. A trailer extension (shown) was also available in Japan. *Courtesy of Orson Christian of CapturedPrey.com*

The combined form of Super Ginrai and Godbomber was known as God Ginrai. When Powermaster Optimus Prime was reissued by Hasbro in 2003, this Japanese version was used and not the original Hasbro version. *Courtesy of Orson Christian of CapturedPrey.com*

In Japan Super Ginrai and Godbomber were sold separately, as well as a gift set. *Courtesy of Orson Christian of CapturedPrey.com*

Powermaster Slapdash with Lube.

Powermaster Joyride with Hotwire. These later characters are not as in demand by collectors, but at the same time do not often pop up for sale sealed. A sealed sample like this can sell for $350 to $425.

Powermasters Getaway with Rev, Joyride with Hotwire, and Slapdash with Lube. *Courtesy of Orson Christian of CapturedPrey.com*

Ranger was the Takara version of Joyride. It was the same exact toy, just different colors and a totally different character. *Courtesy of Orson Christian of CapturedPrey.com*

Decepticon Powermasters Darkwing (with Throttle) and Dreadwind (with Hi-Test). In Japan these figures were never released in these colors; they were different characters named Hydra and Buster, and were sold separately or in a gift set.

Darkwing and Dreadwind had their own vehicle mode, but were also able to combine into a larger jet.

These were the only Powermasters featuring the vehicle combination gimmick. Their combined form was named Dreadwing.

Powermaster Doubledealer sealed can sell for $575 to $750+.
Courtesy of Robert T. Yee

Doubledealer could disguise himself as an Autobot in robot mode, but was in fact a Decepticon [shown with both his Powermaster engines Knok and Skar [the bat]].

Doubledealer's "Autobot" vehicle mode.

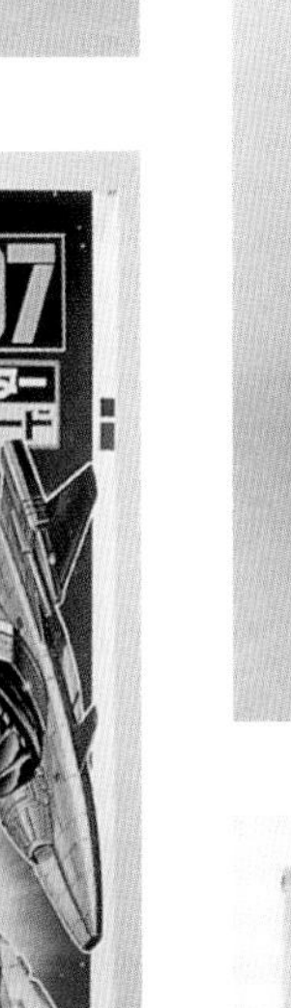

Doubledealer's Decepticon beast mode.

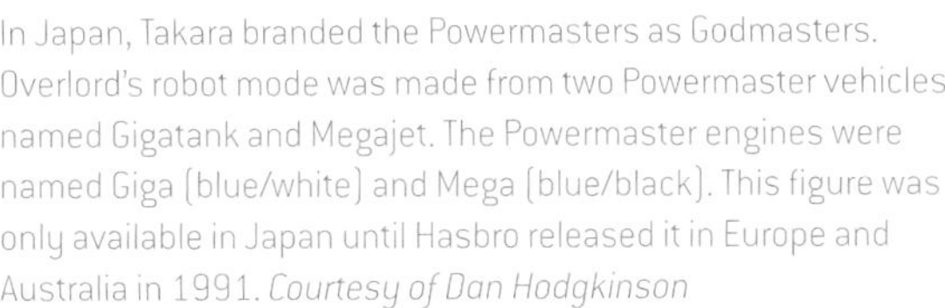

In Japan, Takara branded the Powermasters as Godmasters. Overlord's robot mode was made from two Powermaster vehicles named Gigatank and Megajet. The Powermaster engines were named Giga [blue/white] and Mega [blue/black]. This figure was only available in Japan until Hasbro released it in Europe and Australia in 1991. *Courtesy of Dan Hodgkinson*

The 1988 Small Headmasters and Targetmasters were able to share their heads or weapons, but were not compatible with their 1987 counterparts (l to r): Siren, Nightbeat, and Hosehead (missing an antenna).

The Small Headmasters still came with compartments or seats for their pilots to ride in: Siren came with Quig, Nightbeat with Muzzle, and Hosehead with Lug.

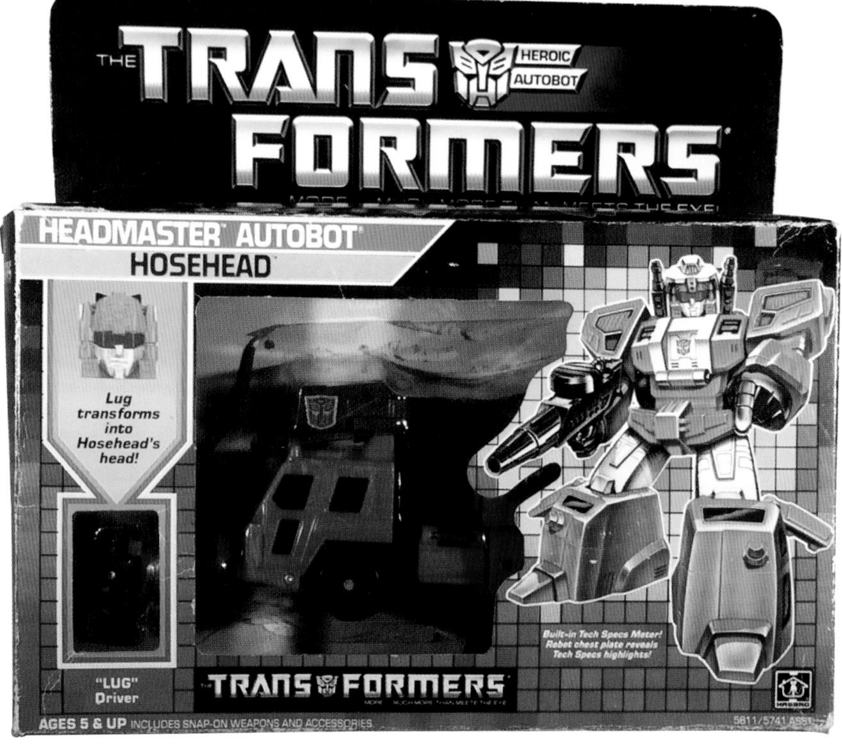

Fangry (with Brisko), Squeezeplay (with Lokos), and Horri-Bull (with Kreb). *Courtesy of Orson Christian of CapturedPrey.com*

Spinster with Singe (black) and Hairsplitter (purple), Quake with Tiptop (purple) and Heater (black), and Needlenose with Sunbeam (purple) and Zigzag (black). *Courtesy of Orson Christian of CapturedPrey.com*

The Small Targetmasters of this year came carded and featured two Targetmaster weapons.

The Small Autobot Targetmasters Landfill with Flintlock (blue) and Silencer (yellow), Quickmix with Boomer (blue) and Ricochet (yellow), and Scoop with Tracer (yellow) and Holepunch (blue). *Courtesy of Orson Christian of CapturedPrey.com*

Cloudburst (named Phoenix in Japan) and Waverider (Diver in Japan). *Courtesy of Robert T. Yee*

The 1988 Pretenders all came boxed, displaying their shell and inner robot in the package. In Japan, Landmine was named Lander. *Courtesy of Robert T. Yee*

The Pretender packaging in Japan had a flip-up panel to reveal a window box underneath.

Pretenders Cloudburst, Waverider, and Landmine. *Courtesy of Ronen Kauffman of toylab.info*

The inner Pretender robots (l to r): Splashdown, Sky High, and Groundbreaker.

Splashdown, Groundbreaker, and Sky High Pretender shells. This set of three Pretenders was never offered by Takara in the Japanese market.

Submarauder (named Gilmer in Japan) and Bomb-Burst (Blood in Japan). Along with Skullgrin, these toys were released by Takara without any significant physical changes—except to the fiction.

Decepticon Pretenders Bomb-Burst, Skullgrin, and Submarauder. *Courtesy of Ronen Kauffman of toylab.info*

Bugly, Iguanus, and Finback were exclusive to Hasbro and not released by Takara.

Courtesy of Robert T. Yee

The Pretender Beasts were also exclusive to Hasbro; in robot mode are Chainclaw (right) and Catilla (left). These inner robots were shorter than the bipedal Pretenders, but had more to their transformations.

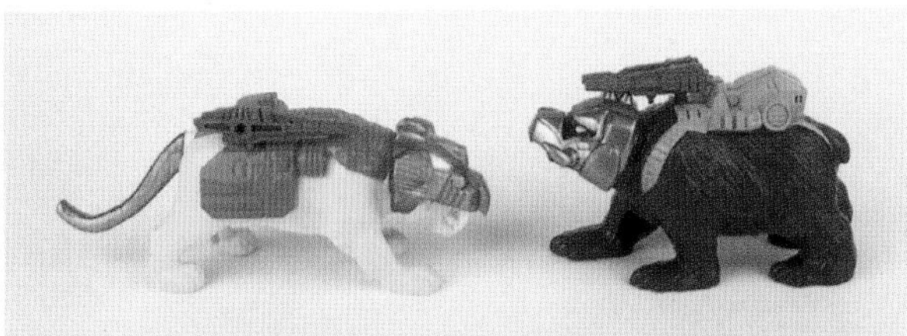

To open the Autobot beast shells their helmets had to be removed.

An exclusive Large Pretender to Japan was Metalhawk. Metalhawk was a central character to the Japanese fiction. This character has since transcended and become part of the Hasbro comic continuity. *Courtesy of Chuck Liu of artfire2000.com*

The Autobot Pretender Beasts seem to be easier to acquire than the Decepticon versions. In a sealed and mint box, perfect samples can sell from $225 to $325.

Pretender Beasts Carnivac and Snarler. *Courtesy of Ronen Kauffman of toylab.info*

Carnivac and Snarler sealed can sell for $350 to $400.

Neither Roadgrabber (shown) nor Gunrunner was released by Takara.

Roadgrabber standing next to his vehicle. When placed inside the vehicle Roadgrabber basically just lays down.

Instead of featuring a shell to hide a robot in, these Pretenders hid their robots inside vehicles. Seen here is Gunrunner, who can sell for $350 to $450 sealed.

Roadgrabber and his vehicle had the ability to transform. Loose, complete, and in mint condition the Pretender Vehicles will sell between $60 and $85. Roadgrabber tends to sell for a bit more than Gunrunner.

The Autobot Sparkabots Sizzle, Fizzle, and Guzzle. *Courtesy of Orson Christian of CapturedPrey.com*

Sealed on the card Sparkabots can sell from $50 to $100, with Guzzle being the most popular of the three.

When pushed forward in vehicle mode the Sparkabots' inner mechanism would shoot sparks out the back (tailpipe sections). *Courtesy of Orson Christian of CapturedPrey.com*

Cindersaur, Flamefeather, and Sparkstalker. The Decepticon Firecons could shoot sparks from their dragon mouths when pushed forward in beast mode.

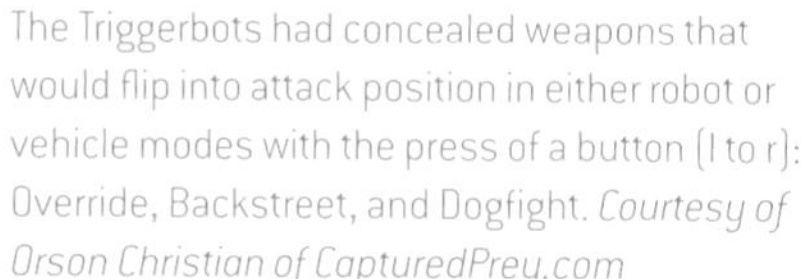

The Triggerbots had concealed weapons that would flip into attack position in either robot or vehicle modes with the press of a button (l to r): Override, Backstreet, and Dogfight. *Courtesy of Orson Christian of CapturedPrey.com*

Triggerbots and their Decepticon counterparts, the Triggercons, can sell between $75 and $135 carded. Shown is Override.

Backstreet and Dogfight. *Courtesy of Chuck Liu of artfire2000.com*

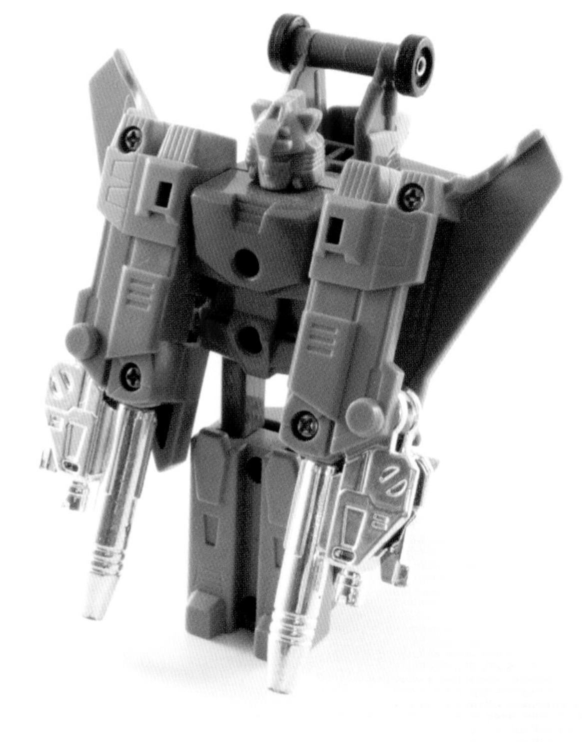

Triggercons Ruckus, Windsweeper, and Crankcase. *Courtesy of Orson Christian of CapturedPrey.com*

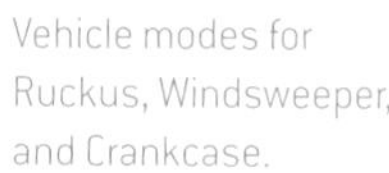

Vehicle modes for Ruckus, Windsweeper, and Crankcase.

Courtesy of Chuck Liu of artfire2000.com

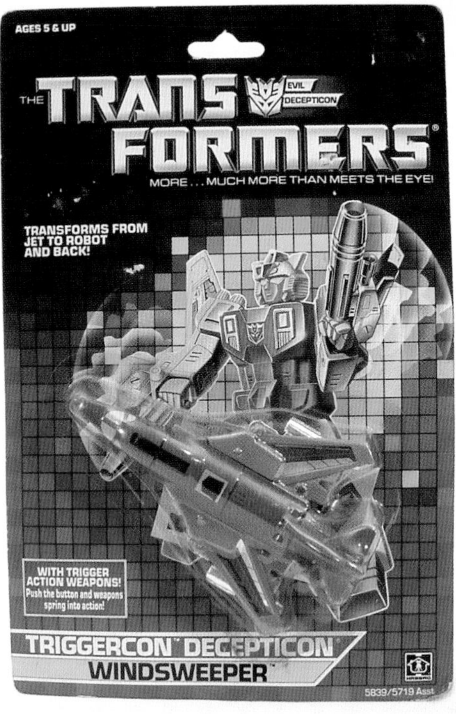

Squawktalk and Beastbox. These Decepticon cassettes each had a robot mode and were able to combine into a larger robot named Squawkbox.

Beastbox and Squawktalk. *Courtesy of Orson Christian of CapturedPrey.com*

Grand Slam and Raindance. *Courtesy of Orson Christian of CapturedPrey.com*

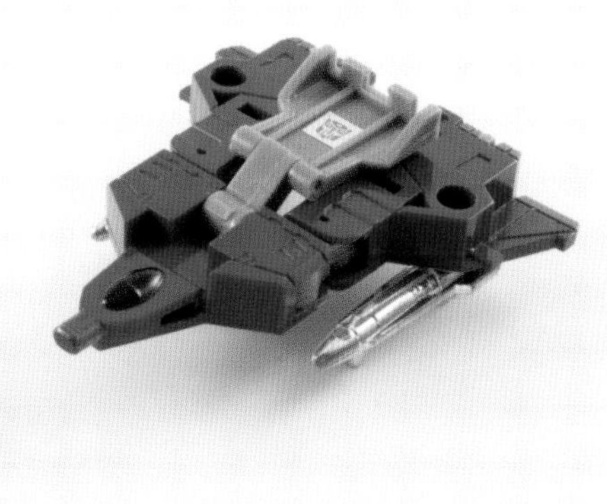

Their combined form Slamdance. *Courtesy of Orson Christian of CapturedPrey.com*

Grand Slam and Raindance could merge into Slamdance. Carded, both sets of cassettes can sell anywhere from $350 to $550.

The Autobot counterpart to Sixshot was named Quickswitch. With a box, a loose complete toy can sell for $100. Although it is quite rare to find a sealed specimen, Quickswitch is not that in demand. A sealed box can still reach between $500 to $850, and sometimes more. For any "professional collectors" or vintage toy dealers reading this . . . ask yourselves when was the last time you saw a Quickswitch *sealed* in the box?

Puma mode

Blaster mode

Drill mode

Robot mode

Boat mode

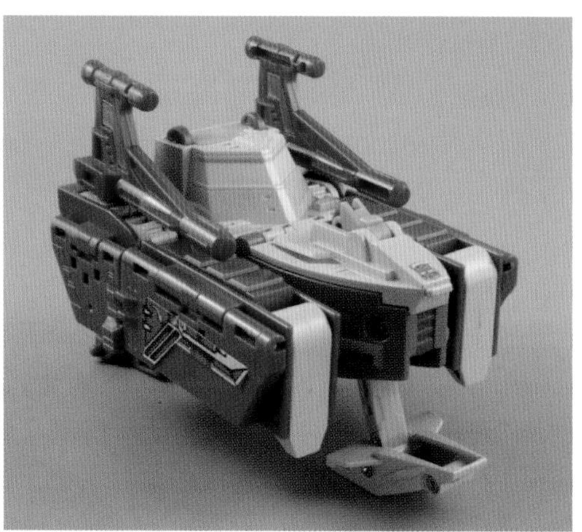

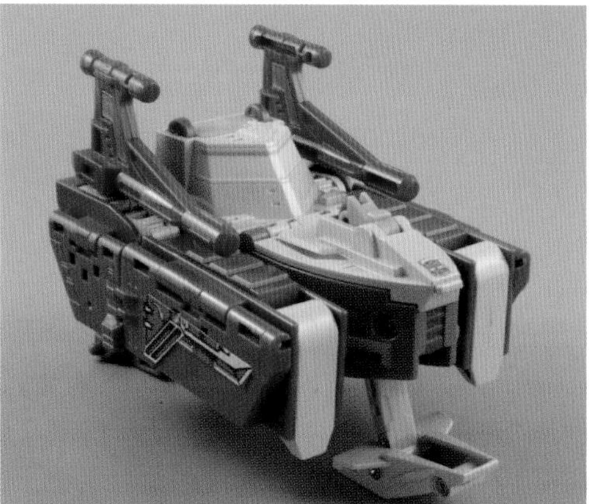

Jet mode

The Seacons were the last standard Combiner Group released by Hasbro during the Generation One period. They shared the same combining design as the previous five-member Combiners, but the Seacons came with five limb-forming members instead of the standard four. Still needing five robots to combine into Piranacon, whichever limb-forming figure was left over could transform into a blaster for Piranacon (l to r): Seawing, Snaptrap, and Tentakil. *Courtesy of Orson Christian of CapturedPrey.com*

Each limb also came with a display stand which could hold the weapon mode of each figure when not held by Piranacon (l to r): Skalor, Overbite, and Nautilator. *Courtesy of Orson Christian of CapturedPrey.com*

The top row (l to r) is Seawing, Overbite, and Skalor. The bottom row (l to r) is Snaptrap, Tentakil, and Nautilator.

Piranacon was also offered in a Gift Set, but the set only contained five of the figures—just enough to form Piranacon. Nautilator was left out of the Gift Set and was only available carded. In Japan, Nautilator was included in the Takara Gift Set. *Courtesy of Chuck Liu of artfire2000.com*

The combined form of the Seacons was Piranacon.

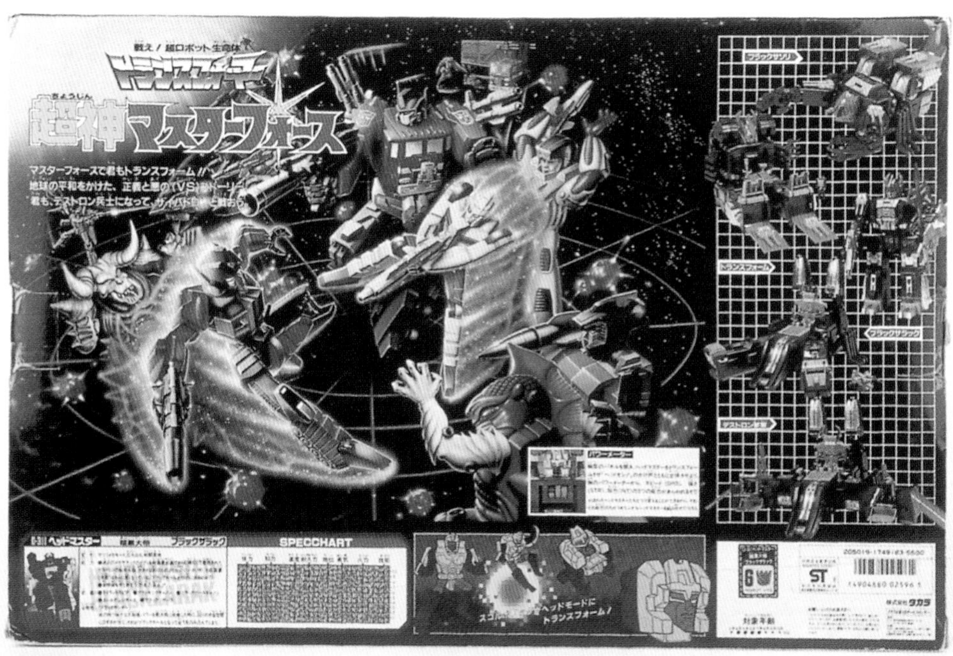

Several figures were retooled and repainted as new characters by Takara. These were sold exclusively in Japanese markets and often cost a premium to obtain. The example seen here is Black Zarak, a Scorponok repaint. A sealed Black Zarak can sell between $6,500 and $8,000+. *Courtesy of Dan Hodgkinson*

Courtesy of Chuck Liu of artfire2000.com

Courtesy of Chuck Liu of artfire2000.com

A repainted Fortress Maximus was also released by Takara named Grand Maximus. *Courtesy of Chuck Liu of artfire2000.com*

Side by side comparison of Scorponok and Black Zarak. *Courtesy of Chuck Liu of artfire2000.com*

A new component was a Pretender shell which his Headmaster Grand could fit in. *Courtesy of Ron Bahr*

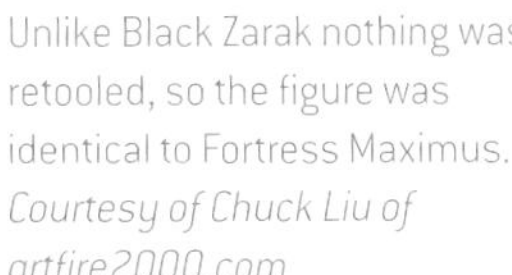

Unlike Black Zarak nothing was retooled, so the figure was identical to Fortress Maximus. *Courtesy of Chuck Liu of artfire2000.com*

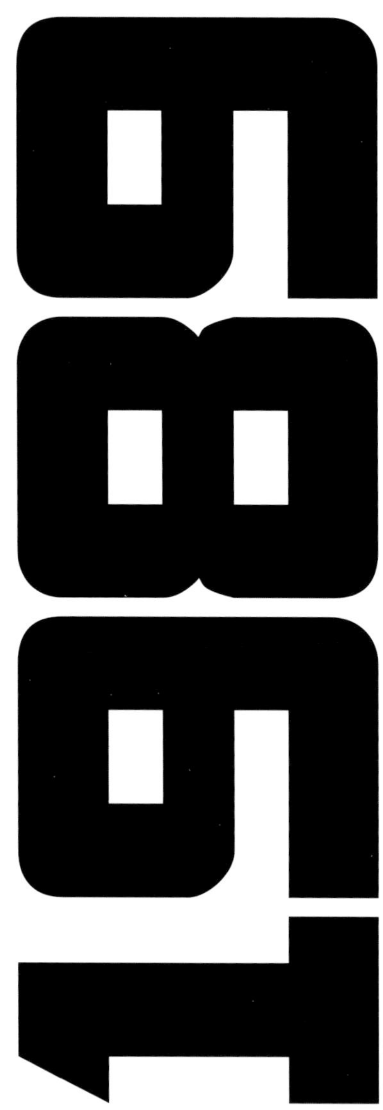

CHAPTER SIX

In 1989, the Transformers line was split between two gimmicks. The first were new types of Pretenders based on the previous year's concept. The second was the introduction of the Micromasters. Because of their small size, Micromasters were able to feature vehicles and playsets which interconnected with one another. Using ramps, the bases could connect to each other to form Micromaster cities. Micromaster figures were sold in themed sets of four figures. Each base and vehicle came with a single Micromaster figure. The Micromasters were all new characters and not new versions of characters from previous years.

1989 CHECKLIST

Autobot Micromaster Patrols (Carded)
Battle Patrol: Big Shot, Flak, Sidetrack, Sunrunner
Off Road Patrol: Highjump, Mudslinger, Powertrain, Tote
Race Car Patrol: Free Wheeler, Roadhandler, Swindler, Tailspin
Rescue Patrol: Fixit, Red Hot, Seawatch, Stakeout

Autobot Micromaster Transports (Carded)
Erector
Overload

Autobot Micromaster Stations (Boxed)
Hot House
Ironworks

Autobot Micromaster Base (Boxed)
Groundshaker

Autobot Large Micromaster Base (Boxed)
Countdown

Autobot Small Pretenders (Carded)
Doubleheader
Longteeth
Pincher

Autobot Mega Pretenders (Boxed)
Crossblades
Vroom

Autobot Ultra Pretender (Boxed)
Skyhammer

Autobot Classic Pretenders (Carded)
Bumblebee
Grimlock
Jazz

Autobot Classic Pretenders (Boxed)
Bumblebee
Grimlock
Jazz

Decepticon Micromaster Patrols (Carded)
Air Strike Patrol: Nightflight, Storm Cloud, Tailwind, Whisper
Sports Car Patrol: Blackjack, Detour, Hyperdrive, Road Hugger

Decepticon Micromaster Transports (Carded)
Flattop
Roughstuff

Decepticon Micromaster Stations (Boxed)
Greasepit
Airwave

Decepticon Micromaster Base (Boxed)
Skyhopper

Decepticon Large Micromaster Base (Boxed)
Skystalker

Decepticon Pretender Monsters (Carded)
Birdbrain
Bristleback
Icepick
Scowl
Slog
Wildfly

Decepticon Small Pretenders (Carded)
Bludgeon
Octopunch
Stranglehold

Decepticon Mega Pretender (Boxed)
Thunderwing

Decepticon Ultra Pretender (Boxed)
Roadblock

Decepticon Classic Pretender (Carded)
Starscream

Decepticon Classic Pretender with Shell (Boxed)
Starscream

Carded Micromasters tend not to sell for very much considering their age. This nearly perfect specimen might sell for $50 to $65. *Courtesy of Robert T. Yee*

Autobot Race Car Patrol comparison between Hasbro and Takara packaging. Even in the harder-to-find Japanese packaging, a carded set will often sell between $40 and $55.

The back of the Hasbro and Takara packaging. Takara used this space to emphasize the interconnectivity of the bases.

Autobot Race Car Patrol (top l to r): Swindler, Tailspin, Roadhandler, and Free Wheeler. Decepticon Air Strike Patrol (bottom l to r): Storm Cloud, Whisper, Tailwind, and Nightflight.

Decepticon Sports Car Patrol (top l to r): Detour, Hyperdrive, Road Hugger, and Blackjack. Autobot Off Road Patrol (bottom l to r): Mudslinger, Powertrain, Highjump, and Tote.

The Autobot Off Road Patrol in Takara Packaging, $35 to $50.

Autobot Battle Patrol (top l to r): Sunrunner, Flak, Sidetrack, and Big Shot. Autobot Rescue Patrol (bottom l to r): Red Hot, Fixit, Seawatch, and Stakeout.

Micromaster Transports can sell between $55 and $75 if sealed on a mint card. Shown are Overload and Erector.

Micromaster Transports Flattop and Roughstuff.

Decepticon Roughstuff and Autobot Erector. The transports would attach to the back of the Micromasters via a peg hole.

Flattop was the only Micromaster who could not tow his Transport; instead, he pegged into the runway. The Transports would transform into vehicles or battle platforms compatible with most Micromaster figures.

Autobot Micromaster Station with Hot House. Hot House was a repaint of the Decepticon Tailwind. *Courtesy of Orson Christian of CapturedPrey.com*

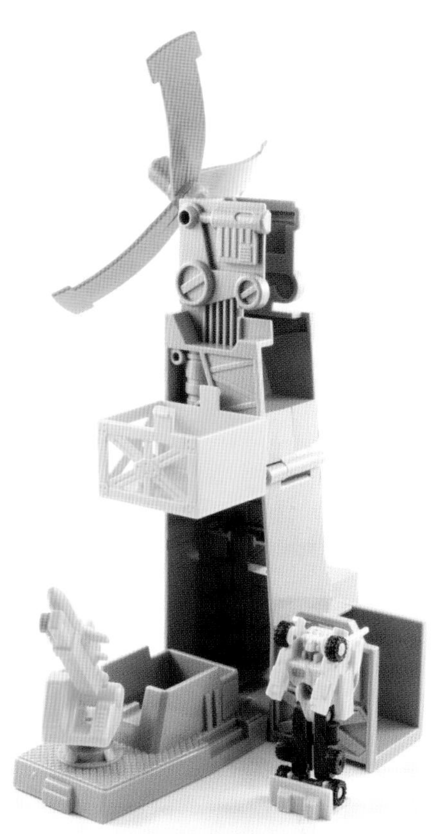

Autobot Micromaster Station with Ironworks. The Micromaster was a repaint of Powertrain. *Courtesy of Orson Christian of CapturedPrey.com*

Decepticon Micromaster Station with Airwave sealed can sell for $100 to $130.

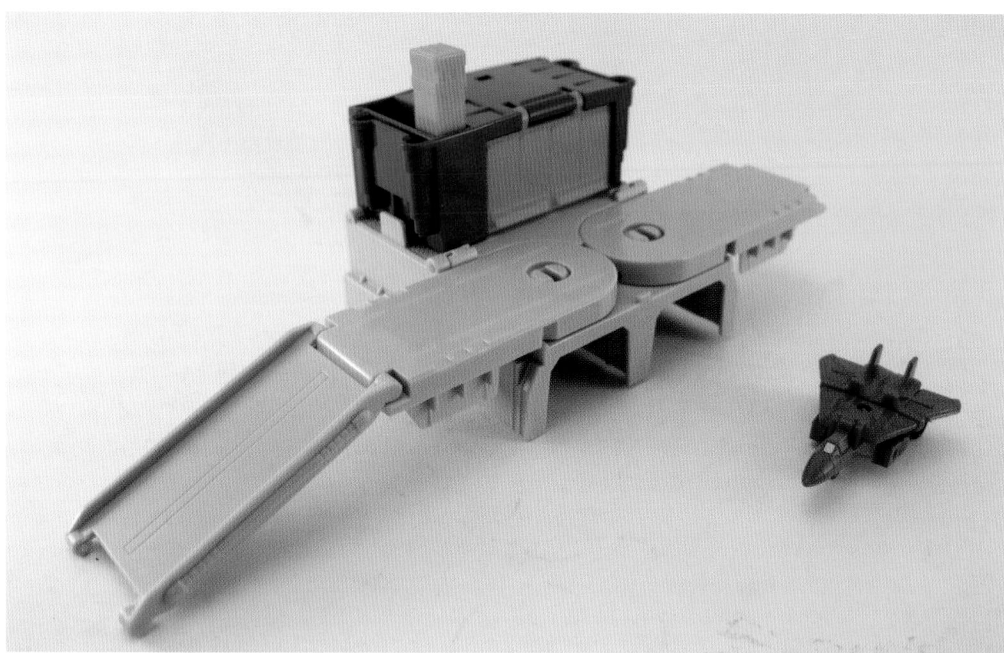

Micromaster Airwave was a repaint of fellow Decepticon Nightflight from the Air Strike Patrol. *Courtesy of Ronen Kauffman of toylab.info*

Decepticon Greasepit.

Skyhopper was a repaint of Storm Cloud. Micromaster playsets came with two styles of ramp: the first type was a dedicated ramp; the second ramp could be connected to another Micromaster playset to form a bridge between the two. Takara's version of this toy came out the following year, painted mostly white and on the side of the Autobots.

Decepticon Micromaster Base with Skyhopper; sealed this item can sell for $125 to $150.
Courtesy of Robert T. Yee

Skystalker with Space Shuttle

Sky Stalker Mexican edition boxed

Decepticon Command Center with Skystalker. *Courtesy of Ronen Kauffman of toylab.info*

This Micromaster was a new figure that would later be repainted by Takara into several other characters, both Autobot and Decepticon. *Courtesy of Ronen Kauffman of toylab.info*

The Autobot Rocket Base was the largest Micromaster playset ever released.

The base came with a new figure named Countdown. This figure never came repainted, nor with any other sets. In Japan the character's name was Moonradar.

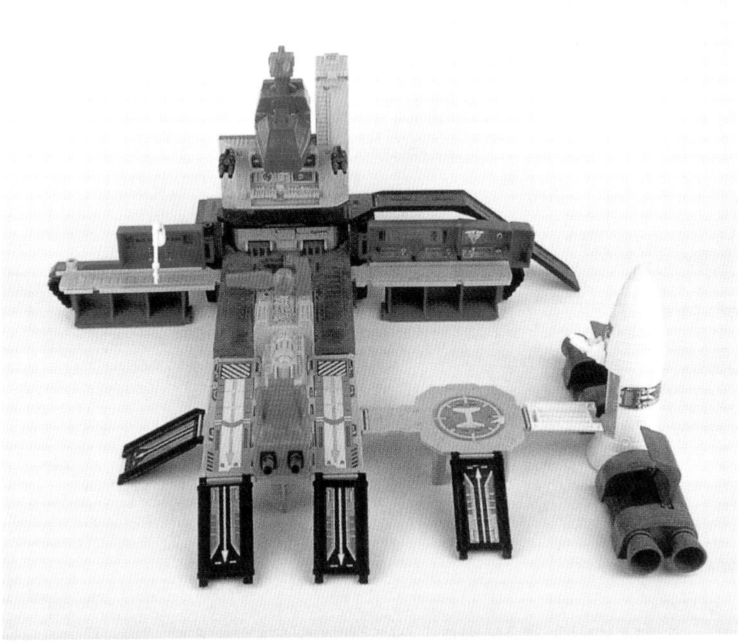

The Rocket Base had multiple ramps and vehicles, allowing for numerous types to set it up. Micromaster bases also came with pegs to plug almost any Micromaster figure into to help them stand.

Seen here are the Hasbro and Takara Rocket Bases. In Japan, Takara released Countdown and the Rescue Patrol as one set. *Courtesy of Chuck Liu of artfire2000.com*

Bristleback and Scowl. The Decepticon Pretender Monsters on mint cards can reach between $100 and $150 in perfect condition.

Decepticon Pretender Monsters (l to r) Wildfly, Bristelback, Scowl, Icepick, Slog, and Birdbrain.

These Pretender shells were rubber, with an opening in the back to plug the figure into. A plastic covering would keep the figure in place and hold any weapons or accessories. Top (l to r): Icepick, Bristleback, and Birdbrain. Bottom (l to r): Scowl, Wildfly, and Slog.

This was the last Combiner Group released under the Generation One banner. Their combined form was named Monstructor.

The Pretenders from 1989 were smaller than their 1988 forerunners, but still featured an opening shell. The Decepticon shells had removable helmets to help keep the shells snapped shut. The inner robots' size and transformations were reminiscent of Micromasters (l to r below): Bludgeon, Stranglehold, and Octopunch. *Courtesy of Orson Christian of CapturedPrey.com*

Because of his prominent role in the fiction, Bludgeon is the most desired of the Small Decepticon Pretenders. On a perfect card Bludgeon will sell for $400 to $600.

Courtesy of Chuck Liu of artfire2000.com

The Small Autobot Pretenders also sported helmets, except for Longtooth (l to r): Doubleheader, Pincher, and Longtooth.

The Ultra Pretenders were large non-transforming vehicles which opened to reveal a transforming shell inside. These shells were on par with the Small Pretenders, such as Bludgeon. The shells transformed into small vehicles capable of holding a small robot pilot.

Crossblades, Thunderwing, and Scoop. The Mega Pretenders were transforming shells which came with various ways to combine with their inner robots. *Courtesy of Ronen Kauffman of toylab.info*

Besides being able to hide the robot within the shell, in vehicle mode the robots could combine to form a larger vehicle with their shells or work individually. *Courtesy of Ronen Kauffman of toylab.info*

The Pretender Legends were characters from early on in the brand (l to r): Bumblebee, Jazz, Grimlock, and Starscream. *Courtesy of Chuck Liu of artfire2000.com*

Autobot Vroom in a better box than shown can reach $500 to $600.

Starscream. *Courtesy of Chuck Liu of artfire2000.com*

Grimlock, Jazz, and Bumblebee.

Pretender shells for Bumblebee, Jazz, Grimlock, and Starscream. *Courtesy of Ronen Kauffman of toylab.info*

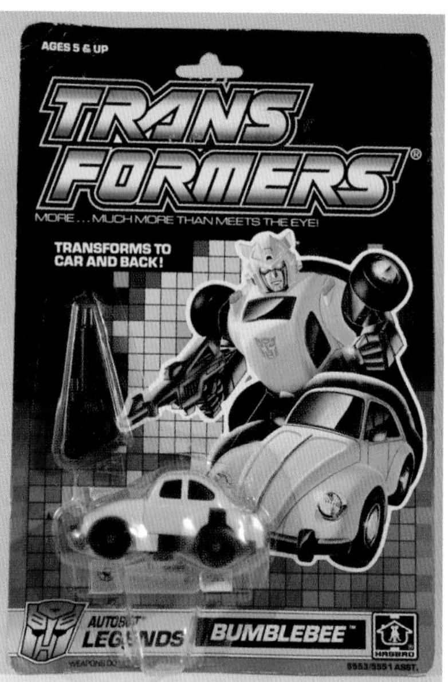

The Pretender Legends were available with their shells in box at all retailers. K-Mart featured the four Pretender Legends robots carded without their shells as exclusives to their stores.

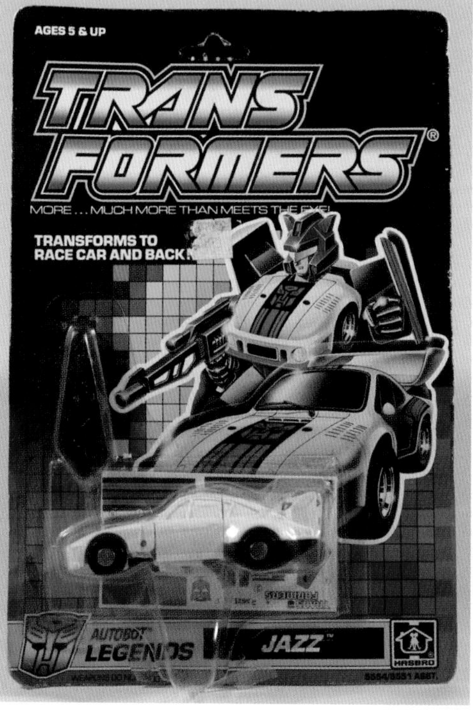

Carded Jazz and boxed Jazz with the shell. *Courtesy of Chuck Liu of artfire2000.com*

Pretender Starscream. *Courtesy of Robert T. Yee*

In Japan, Takara released the four Classic Pretender robots exclusively as a set. *Courtesy of Robert T. Yee*

Continuing the trend of retooling and repainting previously released figures into new characters, Takara produced Greatshot. This figure was made using the Sixshot figure as a base.

One of the new groups Takara released this year were the Brainmasters. The Brainmasters had a small figure similar to a Headmaster pilot that would fit inside the chest of a larger figure. When the chest panel was closed a mechanism would push the pilot figure up to reveal the face of the larger robot. Seen here is Star Saber, who was a double Brainmaster, where the pilot would fit into a large figure, and in turn that figure would fit into a much larger body.

Another exclusive figure to Japan was the Beastmaster Deathsaurus. Deathsaurus had two smaller robots who could transform and plug into his chest while in robot mode. These breast forming characters always had animal forms.

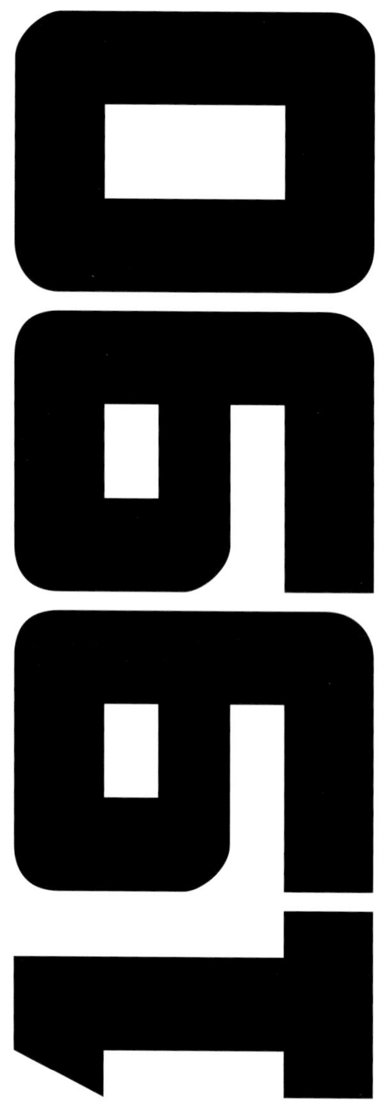

CHAPTER SEVEN

During the 1980s, Hasbro released hundreds of Transformers, but markets were changing, and the decision to cancel production and distribution of the brand in North America was set. 1990 would be the last year Transformers would be released in North America during what has come to be known as Generation One.

Micromasters continued as a staple of the line by introducing new features, such as combining Micromaster figures and combining playsets. The big innovation for the year would be the Action Masters. These figures were comparable in size to modern G.I. Joe figures. These non-transforming classic Transformers characters came with transforming weapons and vehicles to help them battle. The design aesthetic for the classic characters was heavily based on their earlier animation models.

It is almost ironic the Transformers line ended with non-transforming classic characters first released in 1984.

Courtesy of Chuck Liu of artfire2000.com

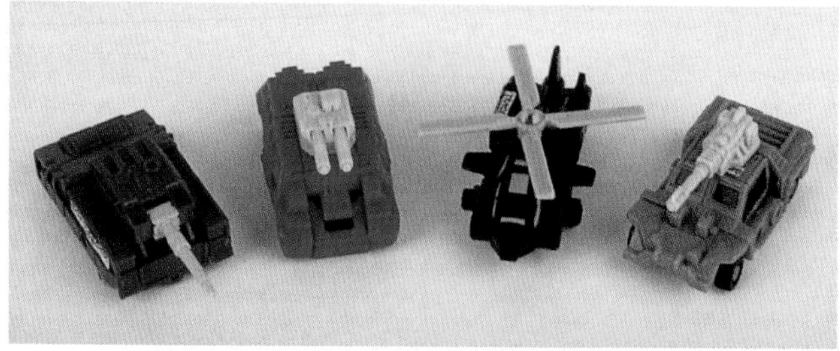

Decepticon Military Patrol (l to r): Bombshock, Dropshot, Tracer, and Growl.

1990 CHECKLIST

Autobot Micromaster Patrols (Carded)
Air Patrol: Blaze Master, Eagle Eye, Sky High, Treadbolt
Construction Patrol: Crumble, Groundpounder, Neutro, Takedown
Hot Rod Patrol: Big Daddy, Greaser, Hubs, Trip-Up
Monster Truck Patrol: Big Hauler, Heavy Tread, Hydraulic, Slow Poke

Autobot Micromaster Transports (Carded)
* With green border around card art
Erector
Overload

Autobot Micromaster Combiner Squads (Carded)
Astro Squad: Barrage and Heave, Phaser and Blast Master, Moonrock and Missile Master
Metro Squad: Power Run and Strikedown, Oiler and Slide, Roadburner and Wheel Blaze

Autobot Micromaster Combiner Transports (Boxed)
Missile Launcher: Retro and Surge
Tanker Truck: Gusher and Pipeline

Autobot Micromaster Combiner Headquarters (Boxed)
Battlefield Headquarters: Full-Barrel and Overflow

Autobot Action Masters (Carded)
Blaster with Flight-Pack
Bumblebee with Heli-Pack
Grimlock with Anti-Tank Cannon
Inferno with Hydro-Pack
Jackpot with Sights
Jazz with Turbo Board
Kick-Off with Turbo-Pack
Mainframe with Push-Button
Rad with Lionizer
Rollout with Glitch
Skyfall with Top-Heavy
Snarl with Tyrannitron

Autobot Action Master Blasters (Boxed)
Prowl with Turbo Cycle
Over-Run with Attack Copter

Autobot Action Master Vehicles (Boxed)
Sprocket with Attack Cruiser
Wheeljack with Turbo Raser

Autobot Action Master Armored Convoy (Boxed)
Optimus Prime with Armored Convoy

Decepticon Micromaster Patrols (Carded)
Race Track Patrol: Barricade, Groundhog, Motorhead, Roller Force
Military Patrol: Bombshock, Dropshot, Growl, Tracer

Decepticon Micromaster Transports (Carded)
* With green border around card art
Flattop
Roughstuff

Decepticon Micromaster Combiner Squads (Carded)
Battle Squad: Direct-Hit and Power Punch, Meltdown and Half-Track, Fireshot and Vanquish
Constructor Squad: Grit and Knockout, Stonecruncher and Excavator, Sledge and Hammer

Decepticon Micromaster Combiner Transport (Boxed)
Cannon Transport: Cemment-Head and Terror-Tread

Decepticon Micromaster Combiner Headquarters (Boxed)
Anti-Aircraft Base: Blackout and Spaceshot

Decepticon Action Masters (Carded)
Banzai-Tron with Razor-Sharp
Devastator with Scorpulator
Krok with Gatoraider
Shockwave with Fistfight
Soundwave with Wingthing
Treadshot with Catgut

Decepticon Action Master Blasters (Boxed)
Axer with Off-Road Cycle
Starscream with Turbo Jet

Decepticon Action Master Attack Vehicles (Boxed)
Gutcruncher with Stratotronic Jet
Megatron with Neutro-Fusion Tank

Autobot Hot Rod Patrol (top l to r): Hubs, Trip-up, Big Daddy, and Greaser. Autobot Monster Truck Patrol (bottom l to r): Hydraulic, Heavy Tread, Slow Poke, and Big Hauler.

International packaging for the Hot Rod Patrol and Monster Truck Patrol. *Courtesy of Chuck Liu of artfire2000.com*

These Micromaster four packs can sell between $50 and $75.

Autobot Construction Patrol (top l to r): Takedown, Groundpounder, Neutro, and Crumble. Decepticon Race Track Patrol (bottom l to r): Groundhog, Motorhead, Barricade, and Roller Force.

The Autobot Air Patrol in robot mode (l to r): Sky High, Blaze Master, Treadbolt, and Eagle Eye. *Courtesy of Ronen Kauffman of toylab.info*

The Combiner Squads featured six robots; one would form the front of the vehicle and the other the back. Each Combiner Squad figure was able to connect to form new vehicles. The Decepticon Constructor Squad (top): Excavator, Stonecruncher, Knockout, Grit, and (bottom) Hammer and Sledge.

The Decepticon Constructor Squad.

Micromaster Combiner Squads can sell between $100 and $150 on mint cards.

The Decepticon Battle Squad (top l to r): Half-Track, Meltdown, Power Punch, Direct-Hit, and (bottom l to r) Vanquish and Fireshot.

The Autobot Metro Squad

Each Combiner Squad consisted of six figures. Each was able to interlock in sets of two to form new vehicles. In robot mode (l to r) are Power Run, Strikedown, Wheel Blaze, Roadburner, Slide, and Oiler. *Courtesy of Ronen Kauffman of toylab.info*

Any Micromaster Combiner could connect to the front or back of a Transport. Autobot Tanker Transport with Gusher (left) and Pipeline (right) were repaints of Decepticons Knockout and Grit.

Autobot Astro Squad (l to r): Moonrock, Missile Master, Phaser, Blast Master, Barrage, and Heave. *Courtesy of Ronen Kauffman of toylab.info*

The Decepticon Cannon Transport. *Courtesy of Ronen Kauffman of toylab.info*

This set came with Terror-Tread (left) and Cement-Head (right). These figures were repaints of fellow Decepticons Hammer and Sledge. *Courtesy of Ronen Kauffman of toylab.info*

The Micromaster Combiner Transports will sell between $150 and $200 sealed in the package.

The Micromaster Combiner Transports each came with a set of interlocking Micromasters. The basic sets came with repaints of existing figures. *Courtesy of Ronen Kauffman of toylab.info*

Each transport had the ability to become a battle station and connect to other Micromaster bases using the ramps. They also had the ability to split in two and become their own vehicles. This set came with Retro (left) and Surge (right), which were repaints of Autobots Stonecruncher and Excavator from the Construction Squad. *Courtesy of Ronen Kauffman of toylab.info*

The Micromaster Combiner Headquarters consisted of a large vehicle which could split apart into two separate vehicles with cockpits for Micromaster figures.

The Decepticon Anti-Aircraft Base will sell between $200 and $300 sealed.

The Combiner Headquarters (Mexican edition—Cuartel General).

The Anti-Aircraft Base came with exclusive combining Micromasters Spaceshot (left) and Blackout (right). *Courtesy of Ronen Kauffman of toylab.info*

The Action Masters featured new and classic characters. Each basic figure was released carded and came with a small transforming animal or small vehicle which transformed into a weapon (l to r): Mainframe, Skyfall, Rad, Rollout, and Jackpot. Bottom (l to r): Bumblebee, Inferno, Snarl, Grimlock, Blaster, and Jazz.

Action Master Blaster with Flight-Pack. Most figures will sell between $70 and $85 on a mint card.

Action Master Skyfall with Top-Heavy

The Action Masters were exclusive to Hasbro and never released by Takara (top l to r): Shockwave, Devastator, and Soundwave; bottom (l to r): Banzai-Tron, Krok, and Treadshot.

Action Master Snarl with Tyrannitron

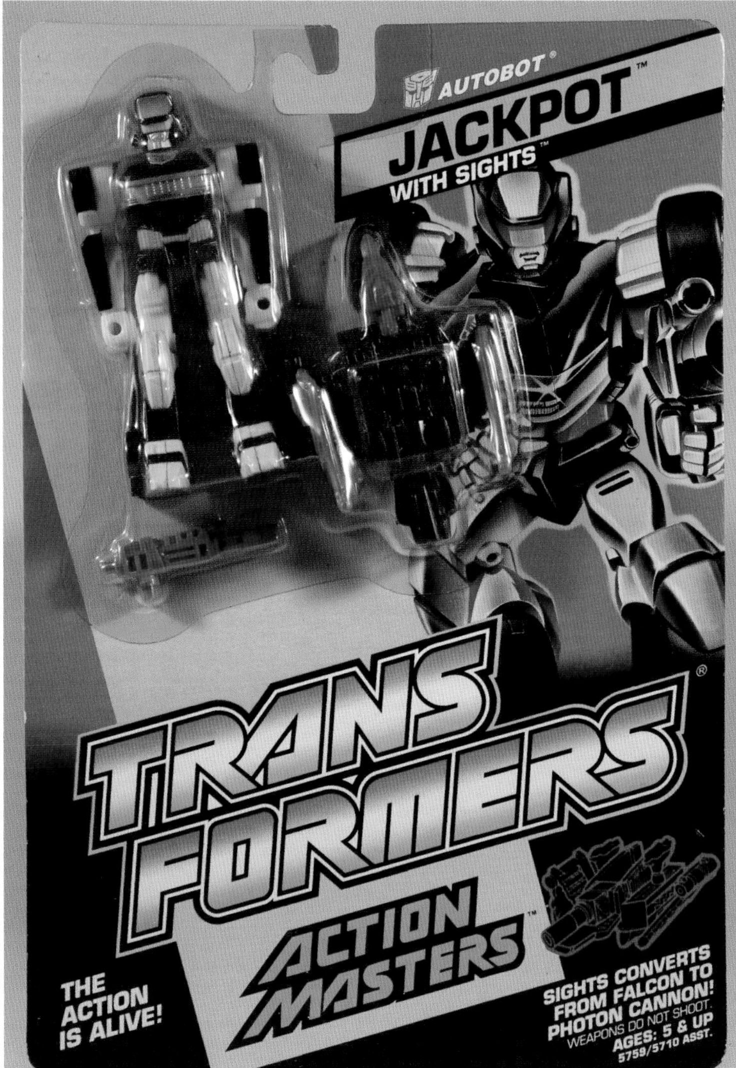

Action Master Jackpot with Sights

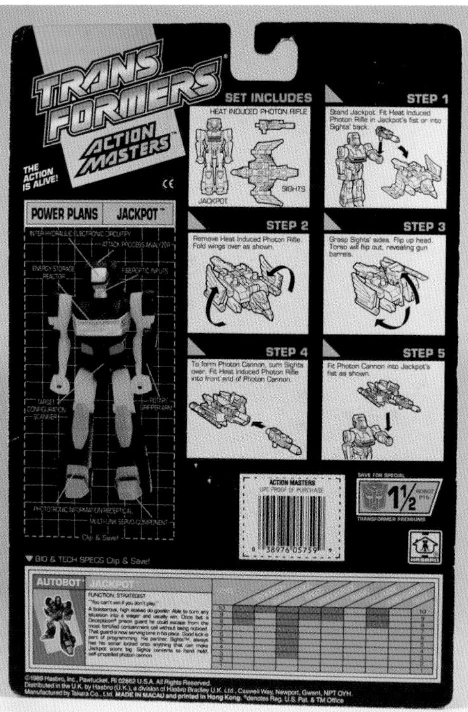

Action Master Kick-Off with Turbo-Pack

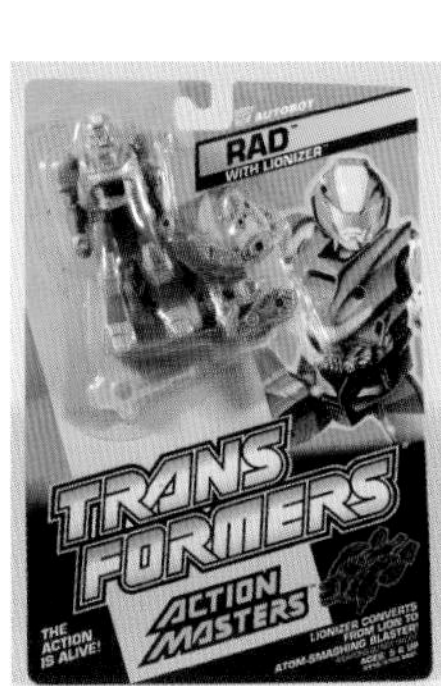

Action Master Rad with Lionizer

Action Master Bumblebee with Heli-Pack

Action Master Inferno with Hydro-Pack

Action Master Banzai-Tron with Razor-Sharp

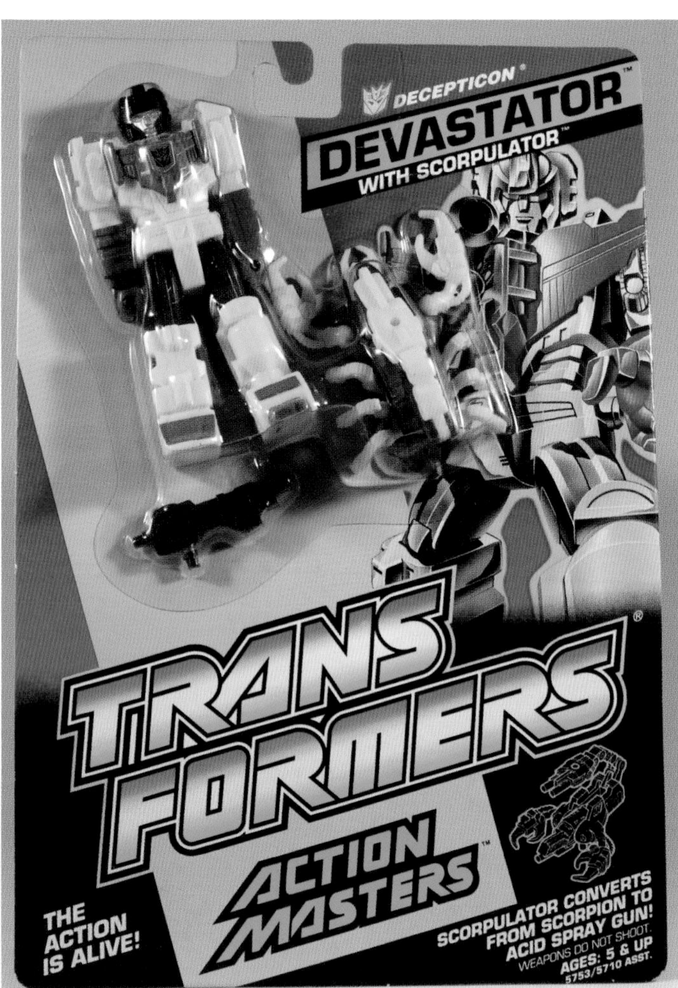

Action Master Devastator with Scorpulator

Action Master Treadshot with Catgut

Action Master Krok with Gatoraider

Action Master Soundwing with Wingthing

Off-Road Cycle with Axer

Attack Copter with Over-Run. Sealed Action Master Blasters can sell between $95 and $150, depending on the character. The classic characters tend to sell for more.

The Blaster vehicle assortment are small transports which transform into battle stations or armor and can work with any Action Master figure. Shown is Axer.

The plastic on some of these vehicles can become very brittle and break if pressured. Shown is Prowl with his Turbo Cycle.

Sprocket with Attack Cruiser

Action Master Vehicle Turbo Racer with Wheeljack

Despite being a new character to the brand, Action Master Gutcruncher with his Stratotronic Jet is difficult to find and in demand; it can reach between $200 and $260+ sealed.

Gutcruncher's Stratotronic Jet transforms into a combat base with a detachable drone and tank vehicle capable of fitting most Action Master figures.

Action Master Optimus Prime—Canadian Edition Box.
Courtesy of Chuck Liu of artfire2000.com

1991 THE IN-BETWEEN

Action Master Thundercracker came with the Solo Mission Jet Plane Exo-Suit. The Thundercracker figure was a repaint of Action Master Starscream. While the classic Action Masters were based off their original color schemes, Thundercracker sported a whole new paint job.

By 1991, the Transformers line was discontinued in North America, but Hasbro still produced Transformers toys in Europe and Australia, while Takara continued the line in Japan. Hasbro-produced figures continued the line where the Action Masters left off. In Japan, Takara was deep into their own version of the fiction, having produced four television series past where the Hasbro season three show left off. Beyond that, numerous Manga comics were released with stories and characters based off figures Hasbro would never release anywhere. These are the figures released in the gray area before Generation 2 began.

This Exo-Suit allowed any Action Master figure to fit inside. It also transformed into a vehicle for a figure to ride on.

Circuit came with the Supersonic Racing Car Exo-Suit.

Autobot Rumbler came with a motorized Exo-Suit (front and rear view of the box). In a sealed and mint box an Exo-Suit can sell for $250 to $300.

This Exo-Suit was compatible with any Action Master figure. As the vehicle rolled forward, the weapons plugged into the front wheels would spin. The weapons that plug into the ports of these vehicles are extremely fragile.

Decepticon Slicer was a repaint of Action Master Wheeljack. The 4WD Assault Vehicle he came with was a repaint and slight retool of Rumbler's Exo-Suit.

Action Masters that came individually carded included Tack-Off with Screech, Charger with Fire Beast, and Bombshell with Needler. These figures' companion accessories transformed into helmets for the Action Master characters.

The three European exclusive Autobots who came individually carded were Sideswipe with Vanguard, Powerflash with Road Rocket, and Tracks with Basher. Tracks was designed to be part of the US market and his original accessory was a transforming speedboat. *Courtesy of George Hubert*

The Action Master Elites were Action Masters who could transform (somewhat defeating the purpose of being an Action Master)—shown are Windmill and Omega Spreem. Omega Spreem's control art did have the name Omega Supreme on it, but somewhere along the line the name was changed, or someone misspelled the name prior to manufacturing. *Courtesy of Chuck Liu of artfire2000.com*

Turbo Master seems to share a lot of similarities with Bruticus. More than likely this was supposed to be an Action Master version of Bruticus. *Courtesy of Chuck Liu of artfire2000.com*

The Action Master Elites all appeared to be inspired by previous characters. Double Punch was clearly inspired by the Decepticon Headmaster character Scorponok. *Courtesy of Chuck Liu of artfire2000.com*

The Constructicons were also rereleased at this time. Not to be confused with his Generation 2 version, this Scrapper had a gray canopy. The card backs were all the same front and back. The back featured instructions for all six Constructicons.

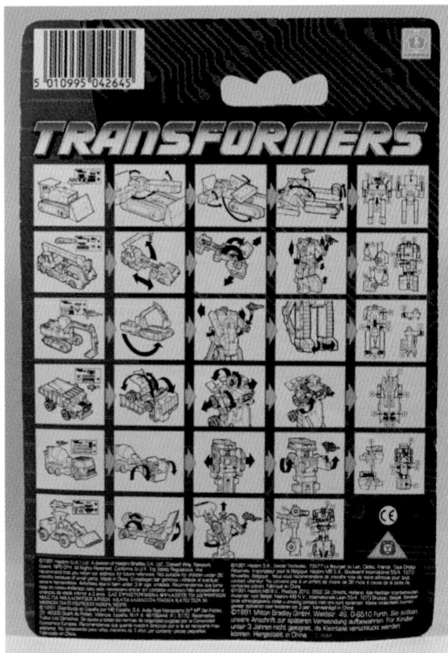

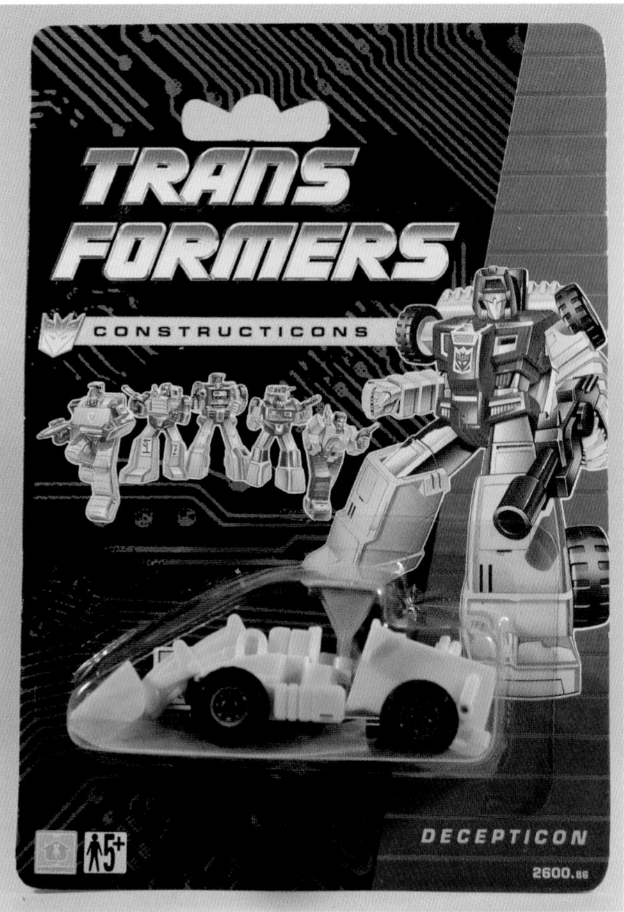

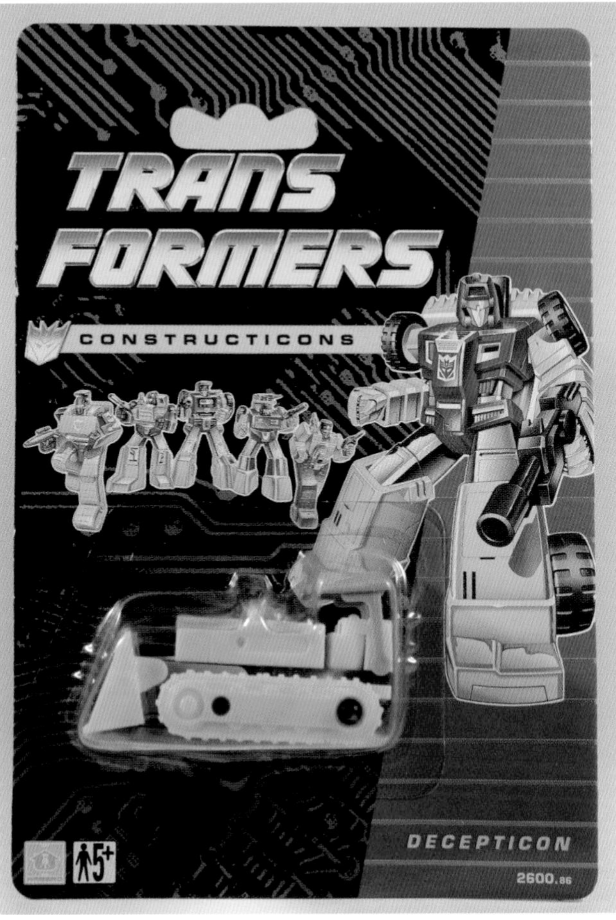

Nowhere on the package did the individual names of the characters appear. These versions also lacked the components necessary to merge into Devastator.

Another Combiner Group repainted and rereleased at this time was the Rescue Force: four figures from the six-member Decepticon Breastforce Liokaiser group originally produced by Takara and released solely in Japan. These characters did not have names and were released as Autobots.

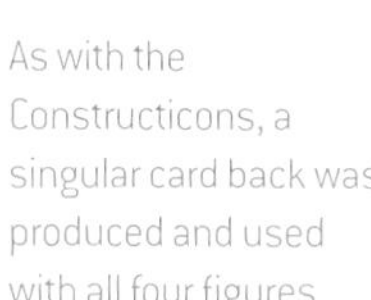

As with the Constructicons, a singular card back was produced and used with all four figures.

Flash belonged to an Autobot group called the Turbomasters. For these basic figures, the small Turbomasters' engines became the robot forms' weapon. Carded these figures can sell between $75 and $135.

New figures included a group called the Predators. This is Falcon, who came with a Megavisor targeting slide. When plugged into a larger Predator figure the slide was visible through the viewfinder. The small Predator jets were never released in North America.

Stalker was a larger member of the Predators. His rocket had a port by which the Megavisor targeting slide of the small Predator jets could be viewed. Eventually this figure was released in North America as Machine Wars Soundwave. Rotorstorm was one of the Turbomasters and was later released as Sandstorm in Machine Wars. *Courtesy of Benson Yee*

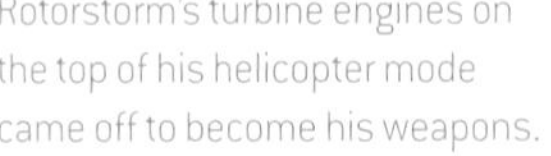

Rotorstorm's turbine engines on the top of his helicopter mode came off to become his weapons.

Crash (who was later rereleased as the more popular Skyquake) also featured the same scope master as Stalker. *Courtesy of Robert T. Yee*

Thunder Clash was the leader of the Turbomasters. Like Optimus Prime, this figure had a trailer which transformed into a battle station. This figure would eventually become Machine Wars Optimus Prime.

Takara had been producing Transformer Jr versions for several years. These were scaled down versions of more popular characters and were designed with simple transformations. In 1991, Takara released a three-pack featuring Chromedome, Optimus Prime, and Fortress Maximus.

These toys retained their basic transformations from their regular scaled figures but were slightly simplified (l to r): Chromedome, Optimus Prime (a.k.a. Convoy), and Fortress Maximus. The trailer for Optimus Prime is actually made from paper.

Here is the comparison between the TF Jr toy (left) and the full size Optimus Prime (right).

Metrotitan was released in 1990. He was a repainted Metroplex figure and came with a small ramp which could allow his base mode to attach to any Micromaster playset. He also came with a repainted Micromaster Skystalker named Metrobomb. *Courtesy of Chuck Liu of artfire2000.com*

Released in 1990, Landshaker was a repaint of the Groundshaker toy previously released by Hasbro in 1989. *Courtesy of Chuck Liu of artfire2000.com*

Metrotitan was one of the few Decepticons released by Takara during this in-between time. *Courtesy of Chuck Liu of artfire2000.com*

Takara's Star Convoy from the Return of Convoy line. This was a reborn Optimus Prime. *Courtesy of Orson Christian of CapturedPrey.com*

Having never released Action Masters in Japan, Takara continued the Micromaster toy line. Takara introduced Micromaster Combiner Teams made up of six figures. Shown are Sixbuilder and Sixwing. *Courtesy of George Hubert*

Star Convoy came with a Micromaster Hot Rod and a Micro Trailer. The Micro Trailers could connect to one another side by side, were spring-loaded, and could fire a Micromaster figure from inside. *Courtesy of Orson Christian of CapturedPrey.com*

This figure featured motorized treads which could roll the figure forward in vehicle mode. *Courtesy of Orson Christian of CapturedPrey.com*

In base mode the motorized mechanism would spin the small black cannon. *Courtesy of Orson Christian of CapturedPrey.com*

The Micromaster Hot Rod figure

From the same line as Star Convoy came Grandus. This figure transformed into a base and could be towed by Star Convoy when in vehicle mode. *Courtesy of Chuck Liu of artfire2000.com*

Also from the Return of Convoy line was Sky Garry. His vehicle form could expand and carry up to three Micro Trailers at a time.

Sixturbo and Sixtrain; these figures were only available in Gift Sets in Japan. It would not be until 2003, when Hasbro repainted and released these figures worldwide.

Several of the Micromaster Patrols not previously released by Takara were repainted and packed with a Micro Trailer. Shown is Astro Squad with Micro Trailer.

Repainted Battle Patrol

Released in 1992 as part of Takara's Operation Combination line, Battle Gaea was a repainted version of the Combaticons. A sealed Battle Gaea gift set can sell between $3,000 and $5,000. *Courtesy of Chuck Liu of artfire2000.com*

Guard City was the Autobot equivalent of Battle Gaea and a repainted set of Protectobots. *Courtesy of Chuck Liu of artfire2000.com*

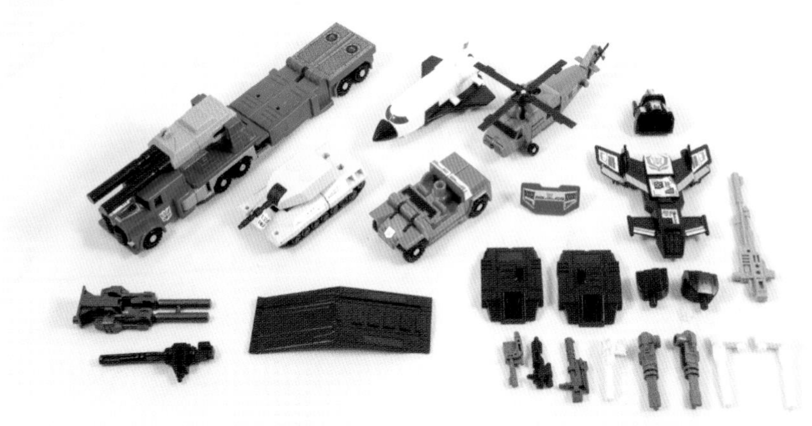

The members of Battle Gaea were Great Cannon (Onslaught), Sandstorm (Brawl), Shuttle Gunner (Blast Off), Leyland (Swindle), and Tiger Hawk (Vortex). *Courtesy of Chuck Liu of artfire2000.com*

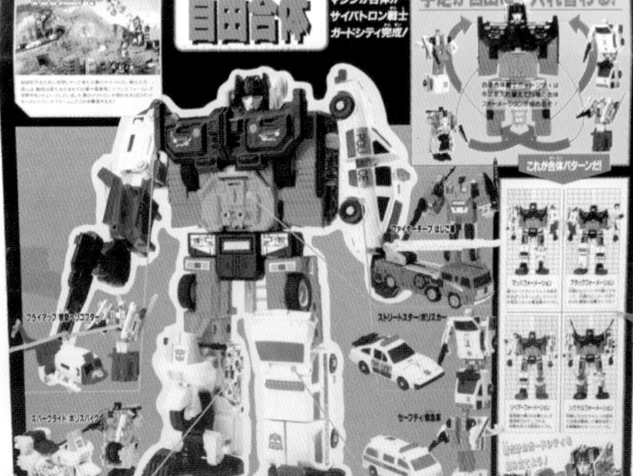

The team was made up of Fire Chief (Hot Spot), Fly-Up (Blades), Streetstar (Streetwise), Safety (First Aid), and Sparkride (Groove). *Courtesy of Chuck Liu of artfire2000.com*

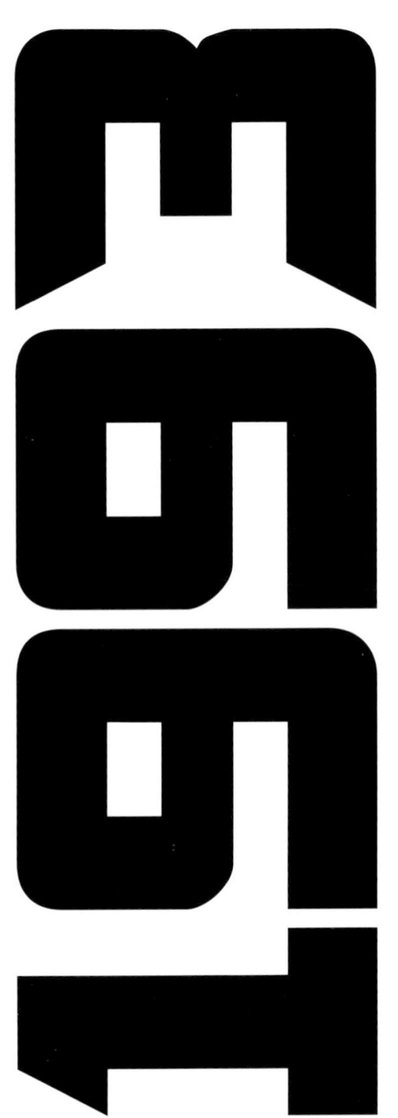

CHAPTER EIGHT

In North America, the Transformers line ended in 1990. In the rest of the world the line continued in various ways. Generation 2 is the official name of the Transformers relaunch, which began in North America and later spread to other markets starting in 1993. The initial figures of this line consisted of classic characters and their repainted Generation One toys with new parts and weapons. During the first two years of Generation 2 (or G2), each figure came branded with their respected revamped faction symbol and faction name painted somewhere on their body.

By 1994, many new figures and characters were being introduced along with several repainted Generation One Combiner Teams. As the line came to a close in 1995, it consisted of entirely new figures. The big take-away from the Generation 2 line is the design direction of using ball joints to give the figures far more articulation. These types of joints would become instrumental in many Transformers toy lines for years to come.

As stated earlier, during the gap in North America between 1991 and 1992, the Transformers line continued abroad. That grey area of pre-G2 will be explored in the next chapter.

Autobot Minicars Seapray and Bumblebee. Both are vacuum metalized chrome versions of their Generation One colors.

GENERATION 2 CHECKLIST

1993

Autobot Minicars (Carded)
Beachcomber
Bumblebee
Hubcap
Seaspray

Autobot Small Cars (Carded)
Rapido
Skram
Turbofire
Windbreaker

Autobot Cars (Carded)
Inferno
Jazz
Sideswipe

Autobot Dinobots (Carded)
Grimlock (silver body, blue body, turquoise body)
Slag (silver body, red body, green body)
Snarl (silver body, red body, green body)

Autobot Color Changers (Carded)
Drench
GoBots

Autobot Leader (Boxed)
Optimus Prime

Decepticon Constructicons (Carded)
*Both orange and yellow bodies
Bonecrusher
Hook
Long Haul
Mixmaster
Scavenger
Scrapper

Decepticon Small Jets (Carded)
Afterburner
Eagle Eye
Terradive
Windrazor

Decepticon Jets (Carded)
Ramjet
Starscream

Decepticon Color Changers (Carded)
Deluge
Jetstorm

Decepticon Leader (Boxed)
Megatron

1994

Autobot Aerialbots (Carded)
Air Raid
Fireflight
Silverbolt
Skydive
Slingshot

Autobot Laser Rods (Carded)
Electro
Volt

Autobot Rotor Force (Carded)
Leadfoot
Manta Ray

Autobot Hero (Carded)
Optimus Prime

Decepticon Combaticons (Carded)
Blast Off
Brawl
Onslaught
Swindle
Vortex

Decepticon Laser Rods (Carded)
Jolt
Sizzle

Decepticon Rotor Force (Carded)
Powerdive
Ransack

Decepticon Hero (Carded)
Megatron

Other Decepticons (Boxed)
Dreadwing and Smokescreen

Botcon Convention Exclusive (Carded)
Breakdown

1995

Autobot Go-Bots (Carded)
Blowout
Bumblebee
Double Clutch
Firecracker
Gearhead
High Beam
Ironhide
Mirage
Motormouth
Optimus Prime
Sideswipe

Autobot Cyberjets (Carded)
Air Raid
Jetfire
Strafe

Autobot Laser Cycle (Carded)
Road Rocket

Autobot Leader (Boxed)
Optimus Prime

Decepticon Go-Bots (Carded)
Frenzy
Megatron
Soundwave

Decepticon Cyberjets (Carded)
Hooligan
Skyjack
Space Case

Decepticon Laser Cycle (Carded)
Road Pig

Decepticon Auto Rollers (Carded)
Dirtbag
Roadblock

Botcon Convention Exclusive (Carded)
Nightracer

Bumblebee, Seaspray, Hubcap, and Beachcomber

Beachcomber and Hubcap were repainted into new colors.

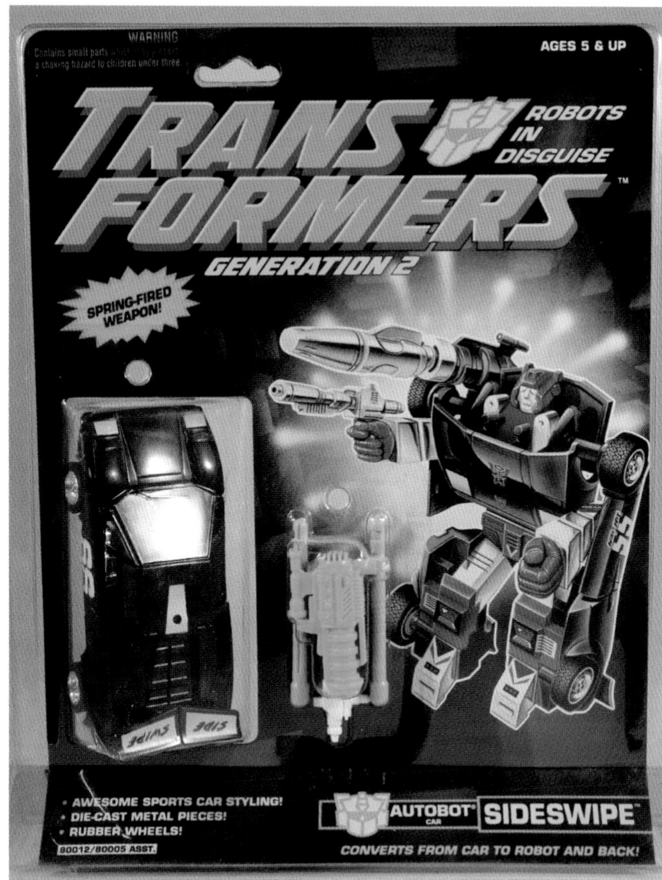

Autobots Sideswipe and Jazz came with new missile launching weapons. Inferno came with a push-activated water cannon. This style of package is somewhere between carded and boxed. It is sometimes referred to as triangle packaging.

The Dinobots were available in three different colors. All three came in silver, which is extremely hard to find. As seen here (l to r) Slag also came in red, Grimlock in turquoise, and Snarl in green. The turquoise Grimlock and green Snarl are the more difficult to find from this set. *Courtesy of Orson Christian of CapturedPrey.com*

The Dinobots were also available in the following colors (robot mode l to r): Grimlock in blue, Snarl in red, and Slag in green. These particular color variants are the most commonly found.

Optimus Prime's new accessories included two spring-powered rocket launching blasters. These could be held by the Optimus Prime figure, as well as connect to another new feature: a speaker box. This black box with a silver Autobot symbol on it connected to the front of the trailer. The box had three buttons, activating lights and sounds including engine noise, firing sounds, and the phrase "I am Optimus Prime."

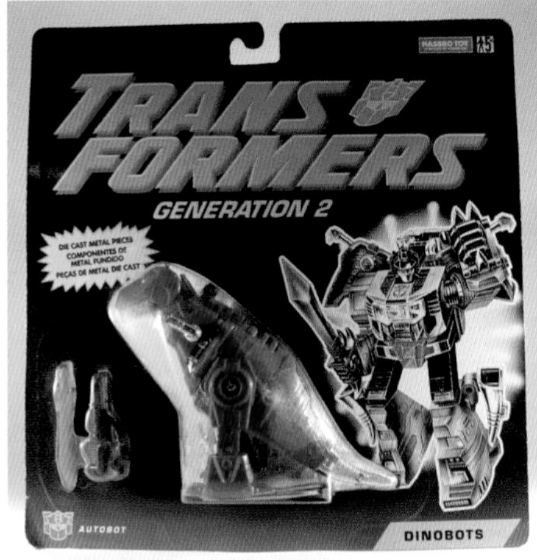

European carded Dinobots came on rather large blister cards instead of the triangle packaging seen in North America.

On the secondary market the Small Autobot Cars can sell between $35 and $40 on mint condition cards.

The Small Autobot Cars were some of the first new figures from 1993 (l to r): Skram, Rapido, Turbofire, and Windbreaker. *Courtesy of Orson Christian of CapturedPrey.com*

The North American and European versions of Windbreaker. In Europe the card back featured the Generation 2 font and logo but lacked the actual name of the Generation 2 subline. Instead of being Windbreaker, the figure was renamed Zap and released as part of the Axelerator group.

Comparison of the North American and European versions of Rapido.

The G2 Color Changing Cars (in robot mode l to r): Decepticon Deluge, Autobot Drench, Decepticon Jetstorm, and Autobot Gobots. *Courtesy of Orson Christian of CapturedPrey.com*

Decepticon Jetstorm and his European Autobot version repainted and renamed Aquafend. Aquafend was released as part of the Aquaspeeders.

The Small Decepticon Jets (in robot mode l to r): Windrazor, Afterburner, Terradive, and Eagle Eye. *Courtesy of Orson Christian of CapturedPrey.com*

The Generation 2 versions of Ramjet and Starscream. These figures came with new spring-loaded missile launchers instead of their original 1984/1985 launchers. They were also slightly remolded to include three pegs which allowed a new light and sound box to attach to the back.

The European carded versions of Ramjet and Starscream. The backs of the package featured English, Spanish, and Italian.

Megatron was an all new figure. In the comic books Cobra Commander had rebuilt Megatron into this Abrams-inspired tank.

This Megatron came with several sounds, such as lasers firing, treads rolling, and the phrase "Megatron Attack!" The sounds could be activated several ways: pressing down the head of the robot, raising his left arm, or pressing down on the cannon while in tank mode.

The Constructicons now came in yellow instead of their original green. Each came carded with all the pieces necessary to form Devastator (l to r): Scrapper, Long Haul, Hook, Mixmaster, Bonecrusher, and Scavenger.

Top: Scavenger, Bonecrusher, and Hook. Bottom: Mixmaster, Long Haul, and Scrapper.

Devastator. None of the Generation 2 Combiner Teams were offered in Gift Sets.

Courtesy of Chuck Liu of artfire2000.com

The Constructicons also came in a much-harder-to-find orange color (in robot mode l to r): Hook, Scrapper, Long Haul, Mixmaster, Scavenger, and Bonecrusher. Individually carded, the orange Constructicons can sell between $70 and $90 a piece. *Courtesy of Orson Christian of CapturedPrey.com*

The orange version of Devastator. *Courtesy of George Hubert*

The Generation 2 Aerialbots. In robot mode (l to r) are Skydive, Slingshot, Silverbolt, Firefly, and Air Raid. Silverbolt sported retooled wings to plug in spring-loaded missile launchers. These missile launchers were the same weapons from G2 Ramjet and Starscream. Much like the 1985 version of Silverbolt, this version did not come with the spring-loaded launcher in his chest. *Courtesy of Orson Christian of CapturedPrey.com*

Generation 2 Aerialbots' combined form Superion.

Each Combiner Group member came numbered on the package. These designations are seen in the lower right hand corners next to the name.

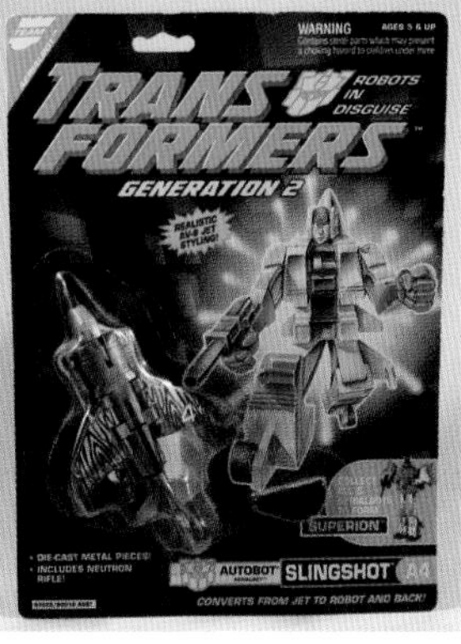

The final Combiner Team released was the Combaticons. Onslaught was slightly remolded to allow for a spring-loaded launcher to plug into his back (l to r): Blast Off, Swindle, Onslaught, Brawl, and Vortex. *Courtesy of Orson Christian of CapturedPrey.com*

Two more teams of Combiners were prepared for release but not put into production. Samples of Generation 2 Protectobots and Stunticons have surfaced over the past twenty years. These unproduced product samples can sell between $5,000 a piece and up. Only the Stunticon Breakdown was produced as a Botcon Convention Exclusive item.

Carded pieces in mint condition will sell for $40 to $50.

The combined form of the Combaticons, Bruticus. *Courtesy of Orson Christian of CapturedPrey.com*

The Laser Rods each came with an LED light in their fists. When activated the light would shine through their clear weapons (l to r): Sizzle, Electro, Volt, and Jolt. *Courtesy of Orson Christian of CapturedPrey.com*

Often triangle packaging will be found discolored and the inner card faded. It seems the packaging just had a way of trapping light and accelerating deterioration.

The Rotor Force each came with a wind-up disc launching mechanism. These could be placed in their hands, while in alt mode the mechanisms became part of their vehicle forms. Shown are Powerdive and Ransack. *Courtesy of Orson Christian of CapturedPrey.com*

Autobot Rotor Force Manta Ray and Leadfoot. *Courtesy of Orson Christian of CapturedPrey.com*

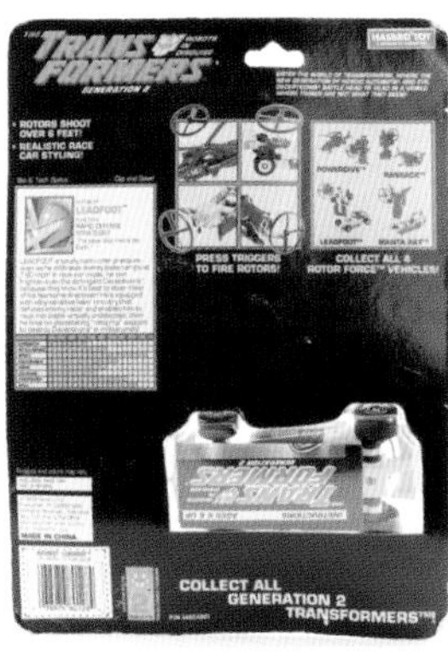

In absolute perfect condition a Rotor Force member can sell between $45 and $55 in package. *Courtesy of Orson Christian of CapturedPrey.com*

Dreadwing and Smokescreen could also merge into a stealth bomber, but Dreadwing could work independently in this mode. *Courtesy of Orson Christian of CapturedPrey.com*

Dreadwing and Smokescreen were new figures for the Generation 2 line. Smokescreen in particular made use of ball joints, giving him an extreme amount of articulation. This type of articulation would become prominent in the Transformers for years to come. *Courtesy of Orson Christian of CapturedPrey.com*

Smokescreen and Dreadwing each had their own vehicle modes: Smokescreen came with spring-loaded missile launchers and Dreadwing came with a H.I.S.S. tank mode. His gatling cannon could hold six missiles, and when the back was turned a pressure mechanism fired the missiles. *Courtesy of Orson Christian of CapturedPrey.com*

Decepticon Autorollers Roadblock and Dirtbag. Several Generation 2 figures came with Pop-up action cards. By folding the card back on to itself the card art of the figure would stand out in front of the background.

Roadblock (left) and Dirtbag had a push transforming mechanism. If pushed forward in vehicle mode they would fold out into their robot modes. By pulling them backward they would fold back into their vehicle modes. Each also came with spring-loaded arm cannons. *Courtesy of Orson Christian of CapturedPrey.com*

Besides Autobot repaints of Roadblock and Dirtbag as Hound and Optimus Prime, two additional Auto Rollers were planed for Generation 2. These figures did not see release as part of the Transformers toy line until years later, during the Beast Wars II Japanese series. Shown are the Auto Roller jet and tank. Both had similar spring-loaded missiles like Roadblock and Dirtbag, but the tank also had a disc firing mechanism. *Courtesy of Orson Christian of CapturedPrey.com*

The Laser Cycles also featured LED lights attached to their arms; when activated they would light up the clear weapons attached. Shown are Autobot Road Rocket and Decepticon Road Pig. *Courtesy of Orson Christian of CapturedPrey.com*

Courtesy of Orson Christian of CapturedPrey.com

Here is a slight variation on the Road Rocket package. The version on the right has a sticker advertising the light-up weapon. *Courtesy of Orson Christian of CapturedPrey.com*

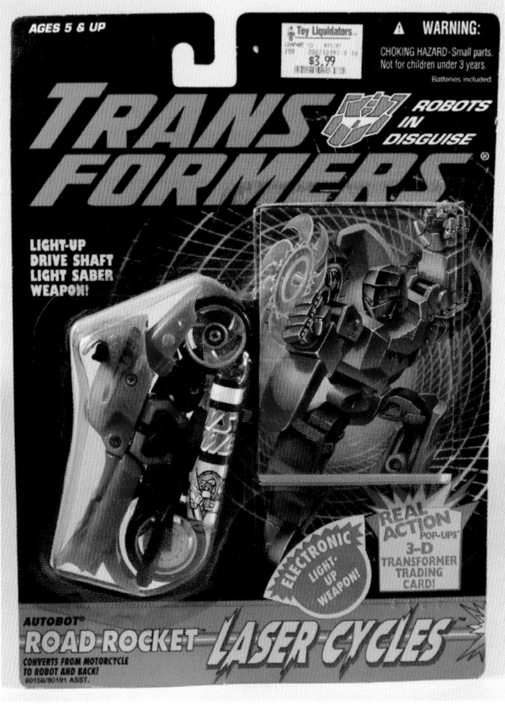

The Cyberjets were extremely posable figures. These figures really represent the beginning of the move from traditional transformation designs to what would be seen in the Beast Wars era (l to r): Hooligan, Skyjack, and Spacecase. *Courtesy of Orson Christian of CapturedPrey.com*

The Autobot Cyberjets made use of the same card art as their Decepticon counterparts, just appropriately recolored.

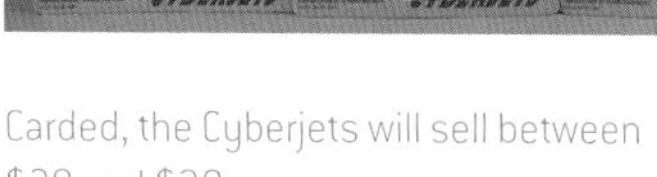

Carded, the Cyberjets will sell between $20 and $30.

Strafe, Jetfire, and Air Raid. *Courtesy of Orson Christian of CapturedPrey.com*

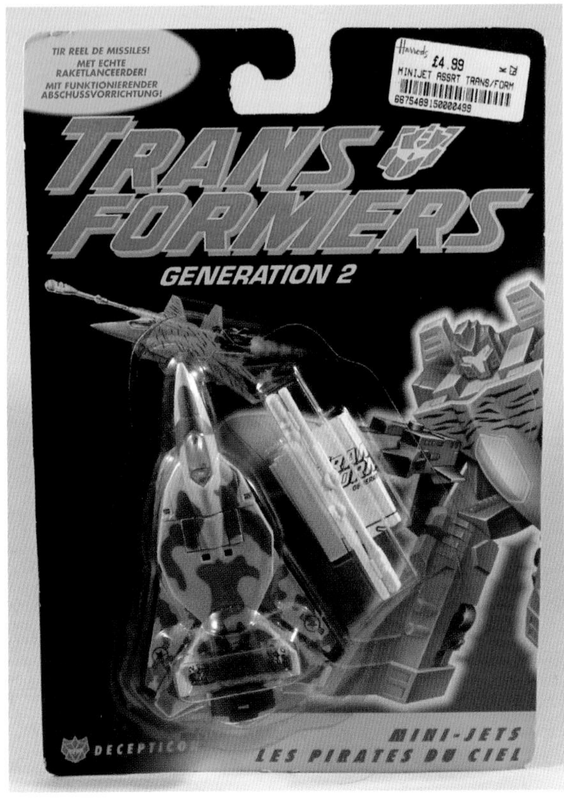

The European versions of the Autobot Cyberjets came with the Decepticon-colored card art on the package.

The Hero segment featuring Optimus Prime and Megatron.

Both figures were extremely posable. Numerous repainted versions of these figures were intended for release but never made it to market. These figures would be used later in various Transformers toy lines repainted and retooled as other characters.

They also came with air-powered missile launchers. By pressing hard on the air pump the missiles would fire. *Courtesy of Orson Christian of CapturedPrey.com*

One of the definitive figures from the Generation 2 line, Laser Optimus Prime. *Courtesy of Orson Christian of CapturedPrey.com*

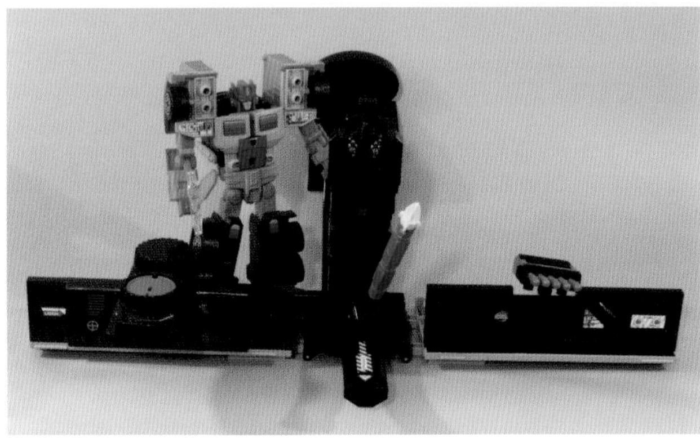

His tanker trailer could fold out and reveal a disc launcher, air-powered missile launcher, and a spring-loaded missile launcher. *Courtesy of Orson Christian of CapturedPrey.com*

This figure featured a great deal of articulation and the light-up laser feature of the Laser Cycles and the Laser Rods. By pressing a button his right fist would light up and allow a red light to course through his sword or blaster. In vehicle mode the same button would activate his headlights. *Courtesy of Orson Christian of CapturedPrey.com*

Laser Optimus Prime in package will sell from $125 to $200. *Courtesy of Duron Land*

Toward the end of the Generation 2 line Hasbro released a group named the Go-Bots. The Go-Bots name came from a Tonka line that competed with the Transformers during the early years of the brand. Once Hasbro acquired Tonka the Go-Bots name officially joined the Transformers Universe. These small figures came individually carded. Some were new characters, while others reused several classic names. Seen here in robot mode (l to r) are High Beam, Double Clutch, Motormouth, Megatron, Optimus Prime, and Gearhead.

Go-Bots Bumblebee. Carded, these figures tend to sell for $15 to $20 on the secondary market.

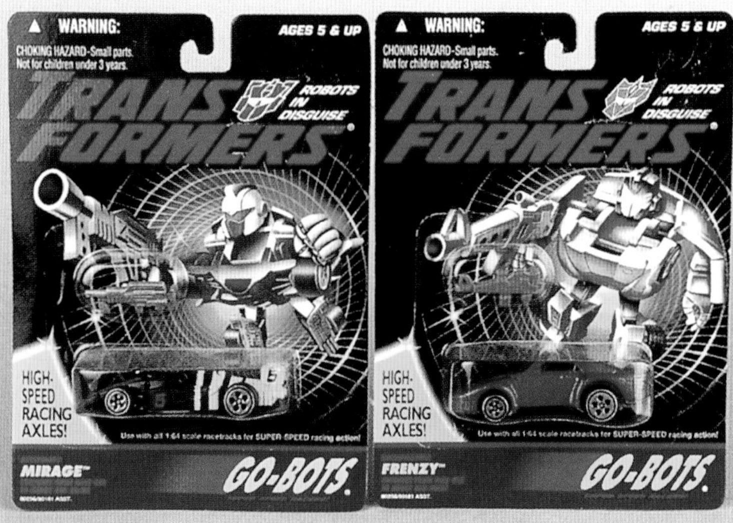

In robot mode (l to r) are Bumblebee, Ironhide, Mirage, Frenzy, Soundwave, and Sideswipe.

Botcon 1995 Convention Exclusive Nightracer figure. *Courtesy of George Hubert*

A second series of Go-Bots was planned but never saw production. These figures did make it to the sample stage (shown). While four of these figures would eventually be released many years later in various Transformers lines, the purple sedan and green Jeep never made it into production anywhere. *Courtesy of Orson Christian of CapturedPrey.com*

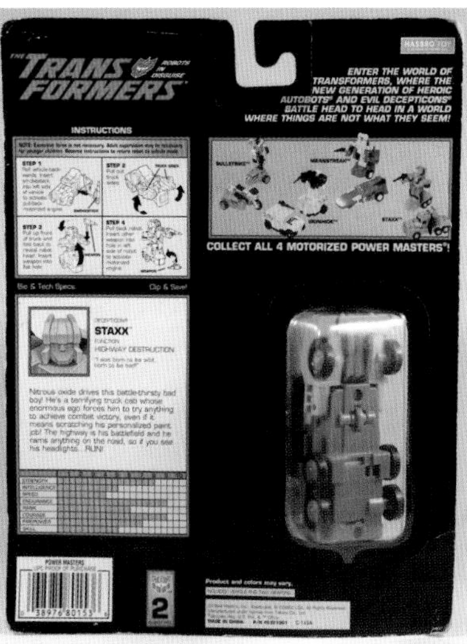

Another group of new figures exclusively available abroad were the Power Masters. These figures had a pull pack mechanism which allowed them to roll forward in vehicle or robot mode. Shown is Staxx.

Obliterators Clench and Pyro (shown) were first offered during the in-between area of G1 and G2. As the Generation 2 moniker took over the brand these figures were renamed and rereleased (but not repainted) in G2 packaging as Colossus (Clench) and Spark (Pyro).

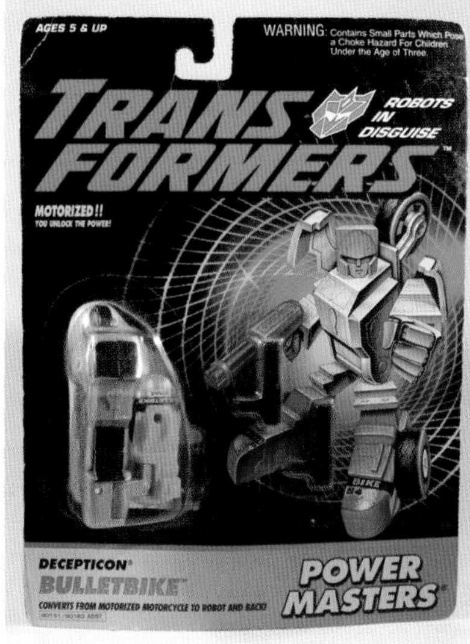

There were four Power Masters, two for each faction. These figures can sell between $35 and $50 on mint condition cards.

Ironhide on a later edition card

Several of the Sparkabots and Firecons were repainted and released outside North America. They featured translucent plastics and retained their spark shooting mechanisms.

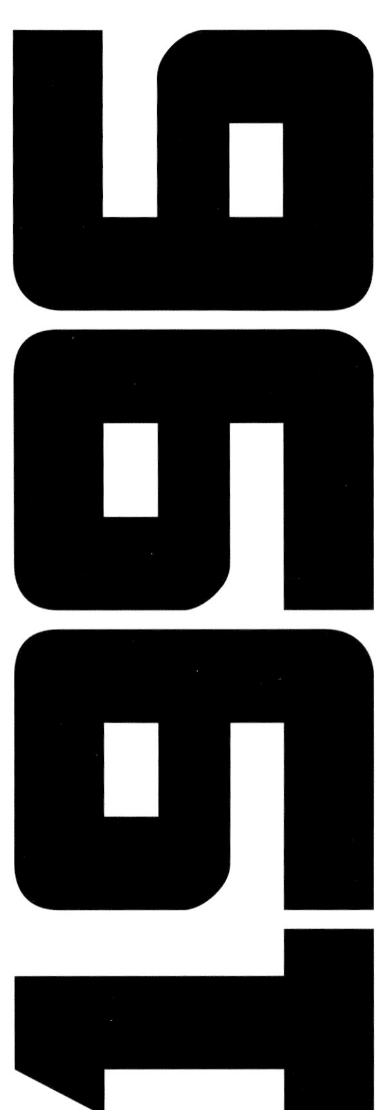

CHAPTER NINE

BEAST WARS INTRO

In 1996 Hasbro, having transferred all boys products to recently acquired Kenner Toy Company, introduced a new series of figures that would once again make Transformers one of the most popular toy lines in the world. The Beast Wars had begun, with new characters and a computer generated television series.

The series continued Hasbro continuity from the original television series with characters that were descendants of the Autobots and Decepticons. Now named the Maximals and Predacons, these Transformers took on alternate modes based off animals. The Maximals were mammals and birds, while the Predacons were insects, crustaceans, amphibians, and dinosaurs.

Often when a new line debuts running changes are made to the figures or the packaging. The first basic and deluxe figures originally came with rock blisters holding the toys on their respected card backs. These were quickly swapped out for the common smooth blister. Some of the first figures of this line were the Basics and had spring-loaded levers that when pulled on would automatically pop up the figure into their robot modes. The initial Deluxe, Mega, and Ultra class figures came with a Battle Head gimmick. This concept was never in the show and was dropped for subsequent figures. The concept was based around having retractable armor for going into battle. Some figures had armor, while other figures had a whole second head stored in their body.

The Beast Wars line was vast, with the last few figures released in 2000. Throughout the time since the line's end numerous reinterpretations of the characters, reissues, and masterpiece editions have been released. This line is a significant part of the Transformers brand. Without this line the Transformers may never have become popular enough to become a feature film. Because the Beast Wars toy line is so huge it cannot be covered in just one chapter. Seen here are many of the early figures released by Hasbro in their original packaging. For an in depth look, including loose toy images, Japanese figures, and merchandise please refer to *Beast Wars: An Unofficial Guide*.

BEAST WARS CHECKLIST

Basic Two-Pack (Carded)

Optimus Primal and Megatron (only available with rock blister)

Maximal Basic Figures (Carded)

Rattrap (with and without rock blister)
Razorbeast (with and without rock blister)
Armordillo
Airrazor
Claw Jaw
Claw Jaw (with VHS tape – European Exclusive)
Snarl

Maximal Deluxe Figures (Carded)

Cheetor (with blue eyes and rock blister)
Cheetor (with red eyes and smooth blister)
Cheetor (with green eyes and smooth blister)
Dinobot (with and without rock blister)
Bonecrusher
Rhinox
Tigatron
Wolfang
Cybershark
Grimlock
K-9

Maximal Mega Figures (Boxed)
Polar Claw
B'Boom

Maximal Ultra Figure (Boxed)
Optimus Primal

Maximal Combiner (Boxed)
Magnaboss

Maximal Basic Fuzors (Carded)
Air Hammer
Bantor
Noctorro

Maximal Deluxe Fuzors (Carded)
Silverbolt
Torca

Maximal Deluxe Transmetals (Carded)
Airazor
Cheetor
Rattrap
Rhinox (dark green body, light green body)

Maximal Mega Transmetals (Boxed)
Optimus Primal (blue body)
Optimus Primal (purple body)

Maximal Ultra Transmetal (Boxed)
Depth Charge (thick box with cluster)
Depth Charge (thin box with arrow)

Maximal Leader Transmetal (Boxed)
Optimal Optimus (with cluster)
Optimal Optimus (with arrow)

Maximal Basic Transmetal 2 (Carded)
* Availabe with II and 2 on Transmetal logo
Nightglider
Optimus Minor
Stinkbomb

Maximal Deluxe Transmetal 2 (Carded)
* Availabe with II and 2 on Transmetal logo
Cheetor
Ramulus
Jawbreaker
Prowl – Prowl colors
Prowl – Smokescreen colors

Maximal Mega Transmetal 2 (Boxed)
Blackarachnia
Cybershark (large warning label)
Cybershark (small warning label)

Maximal Ultra Transmetal 2 (Boxed)
Tigerhawk

Predacon Basic Figures (Carded)
Iguanus (with and without rock blister)
Terrorsaur (with and without rock blister)
Insecticon
Snapper
Drill Bit
Lazorbeak
Razorclaw
Spittor
Spittor (with VHS tape – European Exclusive)
Powerpinch

Predacon Deluxe Figures (Carded)
Tarantulas (with and without rock blister)
Waspinator (with and without rock blister)
Blackarachnia
Buzzsaw
Jetstorm
Manterror
Retrax

Predacon Mega Figures (Boxed)
Inferno
Scorponok
Transquito

Predacon Ultra Figure (Boxed)
Megatron

Predacon Combiner (Boxed)
Tripredacus

Predacon Basic Fuzors (Carded)
Buzzclaw
Terragator
Quickstrike

Predacon Deluxe Fuzors (Carded)
Injector
Sky Shadow

Predacon Deluxe Transmetals (Carded)
Tarantulas
Terrorsaur
Waspinator

Predacon Mega Transmetals (Boxed)
Megatron (purple body)
Megatron (blue body)
Scavenger (with name on leg)
Scavenger (with name on abdomen)

Predacon Ultra Transmetal (Boxed)
Rampage (thick box with cluster)
Rampage (thin box with arrow)

Predacon Basic Transmetal 2 (Carded)
* Availabe with II and 2 on Transmetal logo
Scarem
Spittor

Predacon Deluxe Transmetal 2 (Carded)
* Available with II and 2 on Transmetal logo
Dinobot (off white body) – looking up position
Dinobot (off white body) – straight position
Dinobot (bone white body – only available with 2 on Transmetal logo and in straight position)
Iguanus
Scourge

Predacon Ultra Transmetal 2 (Boxed)
Megatron

BJ's Wholesale Club Exclusives (Carded)
Dinobot and Tigatron
Rhinox and Blackarachnia
Wolfang and Buzzsaw

Toys R Us Exclusives (Carded)
Airazor with VHS tape
Razorclaw with VHS tape
Airazor (Fox Kids Transmetal)
Cheetor (Fox Kids)
Cheetor (Fox Kids Transmetal)
Dinobot (Fox Kids)
Tarantulas (Fox Kids Transmetal)
Waspinator (Fox Kids)

Walmart Exclusive (Carded)
Rattrap

Botcon Convention Exclusives
Fractyl and Packrat (Boxed) - 1997
Antagony (Boxed) - 1998
Vice Grip (Bagged) -1998
Sandstorm (Boxed) - 1999
Windrazor (Carded) - 1999

Microverse Play Sets (Boxed)
Arachnid (with yellow vehicles)
Arachnid (with green vehicles)
Orcanoch

Optimus Primal and Megatron basic two-pack. Seen here is a representation of the rock blister. This two-pack was never rereleased with a smooth blister. This set can sell between $45 and $55.

Insecticon, Armordillo, and Snapper. Non-show basic characters can range from $20 to $25.

Wolfang, Rhinox, and Tigatron. Tigatron was one of the first repainted figures released. There was no retooling of the repainted Beast Wars figures. These were in the second wave of deluxe figures and were never available with the rock blisters. Rhinox and Tigatron, being show characters, will sell between $75 and $100.

Terrorsaur, Iguanus, Rattrap, and Razorbeast were the first four individually packed basic figures. Each had a lever running down the back of their beast mode and ending in the tail. When the tail was flipped up the spring-loaded mechanism would cause the beast to flip into robot mode. Show characters such as Terrorsaur and Rattrap will sell for more at $45 to $50 carded. Seen here are the smooth blisters.

Waspinator, Cheetor, and Dinobot. The first version of Cheetor on the smooth bubble (shown) had red cheetah eyes. These characters carded will sell for $65 and $75 a piece.

Seen here is the rock blister version of Dinobot. Note the darker color on the card back.

Buzzsaw and Blackarachnia. Buzzsaw was a repaint of Waspinator and Blackarachnia a repaint of Tarantulas. Blackarachnia will sell between $75 and $90 carded.

Scorponok had a missile firing pincher and on the other side a robotic bee firing pincher. Another show character, Scorponok can sell for $100 to $130 still sealed.

Megatron came with firing hip cannons and a water shooting blaster inside the mouth of the T-Rex.

Optimus Primal had several features: one arm had a pop-out missile launcher—the other arm a hidden mace—two swords, and spring-loaded shoulder cannons. This figure will sell for $100 to $130 sealed.

Polar Claw was originally advertised for release in darker colors and named Grizzly-1. His front two claws are spring-loaded. One claw can fire a retracting claw and the other a robotic bat.

Airazor and Claw Jaw. These were some of the first basic figures to not feature the spring-loaded transforming lever.

Razorclaw, Lazorbeak, and Drill Bit. Lazorbeak was a repaint of Terrorsaur.

Inferno was the first Mega sized figure not to feature the battle or armor head. Sealed Inferno will sell for $45 to $55.

Spittor, Powerpinch, and Snarl. Snarl was the last basic figure to be released with the transforming lever.

Grimlock, Manterror, Bonecrusher, and Cheetor. This third release of Cheetor came with the green cheetah eyes.

Retrax and K-9

The Microverse sets came with two characters. Arachnid came with an alligator Megatron and a Tarantulas. The Orcanoch set came with gorilla Optimus Primal and Razorbeast.

The only Combiner Groups from the Beast Wars era each came with three figures. Each figure had a beast mode, a robot mode, and combined into a larger figure. Magnaboss was made up of Prowl (lion), Silverbolt (eagle), and Ironhide (elephant). Tripredacus consisted of Ram Horn (rhinoceros beetle), Cicadacon (cicada), and Sea Clamp (lobster). Each set sealed can reach between $80 and $120.

Transquito and B'Boom were Triple Changers. Each came with a third battle type mode. These modes were based around their beast modes.

Transmetal Rhinox, Cheetor, and Tarantulas. Each Transmetal toy came with vacuum metalized chrome. Over time this chrome can chip off even if still in the package.

Toys-R-Us exclusive repaints of Razorclaw and Airazor. Each came with a VHS copy of the first episode of *Beast Wars* season 2 television series.

Transmetal Waspinator and Rattrap. Rattrap is probably the most notorious for suffering from chrome fatigue. Each Transmetal figure came with a slight third mode. These vehicle forms sometimes consisted of minor parts flipping around, while some were more complicated. Waspinator almost entirely transformed into a jet, while Rattrap's legs folded in to allow wheels to come out.

Optimus Primal and Megatron also had slight vehicle forms. Optimus Primal's feet would transform into a surfboard, whereas Megatron had flip up thrusters and fold out roller skates. These versions can sell for $115 to $145 sealed.

Ultra Transmetal Rampage. The early releases came in a thicker box featuring a cluster encompassing the "3 mode conversion." The second and more common version came with an arrow encircling the "3 mode conversion," along with an "expert challenge level" cluster at the top of the box.

Each Transmetal figure had their name written somewhere on its body. Transmetal Scavenger was originally named Inferno, as seen in several advertising images. The first release of Scavenger came with the name written on his leg, while later releases had the name written on the abdomen, where promotional images previously showed the name Inferno written. Sealed this figure only sells between $25 and $35.

Ultra sized Transmetal Depth Charge came in the same assortment as Rampage and shares the same packaging variations, although Depth Charge's second box did not come with the "expert challenge level" incorporated on to it. The thinner boxes were the same height as the thicker versions so the figures were packed tighter in the boxes.

Optimal Optimus was the largest figure released in the Beast Wars toy line. This figure came with electronic lights and four modes of conversion: robot, gorilla, car, and jet. Both versions of the Optimal Optimus box were the same size; the cluster and arrow were the only difference.

Fuzors Terragator and Noctorro

Fuzors had beast modes which were combinations of two animals. Shown are Injector, Sky Shadow, and Silverbolt.

Fuzors Air Hammer and Quickstrike. Quickstrike's cobra tail had a water squirting action.

As the Transmetal 2 line extension began distribution Walmart offered this blue Transmetal Rattrap as an exclusive.

The Transmetal 2 figures intended to display a mix between organic and robotic elements. The early assortments featured the Roman numeral "II" in the logo instead of the number "2."

The logo with the number "2" are the common versions. Here are Maximals Sonar and Optimus Minor.

The extremely rare Transmetal 2 Optimus Minor in blue plastic. Only a handful of samples are known to exist. This item can sell for $1,500 to $3,000. Even though it is quite rare, the demand for obscure Beast Wars items such as this has not quite hit yet.

Spittor and Scarem with the standard logo

Transmetal 2 Dinobot had several variations. (On the left are the differences between the logos.) The center image shows a running change was made to how the figure was packaged. The early versions were "looking up" and the later versions were packaged in a straighter position. Finally, the later waves featured a bone white version.

Deluxe sized Transmetal 2 Ramulus

Deluxe sized Transmetal 2 Cheetor

Later figures like Jawbreaker came shipped from the factories with the revamped Transmetal 2 logos.

Prowl came in two versions. The earlier and easier to find version came in what is referred to as G1 Prowl colors. The second and harder to find version came in G1 Smokescreen colors. This revamped Prowl came in the same assortment as the bone white bodied Dinobot.

Iguanus and Scourge. As was the case in Generation 2, several Beast Wars characters shared names with classic characters. There are a number of reasons why names were used this way, the most common being keeping the name registered to the brand, which requires new products be produced with that name every few years.

Many of the characters which did not receive Transmetal versions were included in the Transmetal 2 line instead. Shown is Blackarachnia.

Another running change was made with Cybershark. The first release of this figure came with a large warning label covering part of the box art. The second release has an adjusted warning label which allowed for more of the box art to show.

Tigerhawk was an unofficial Fuzor in the Transmetal 2 line since the character was based off a merger of Tigatron and Airazor.

Megatron was the only Beast Wars character to receive a new animal for its alt mode. No longer a T-Rex, Megatron became a dragon for his Transmetal 2 toy.

As the Beast Wars line came to a close Toys R Us received several exclusive repaints. These figures advertised on Fox Kids, which at the time was airing reruns of the television series. These repaints were only of deluxe figures. Shown are Waspinator, Transmetal Tarantulas, and Transmetal Waspinator.

During the holiday season BJ's Wholesale Club sold repackaged figures in a cardboard sleeve. Several different sets exist of Star Wars and Masters of the Universe. These are the three sets available for Beast Wars (Dinobot and Tigatron).

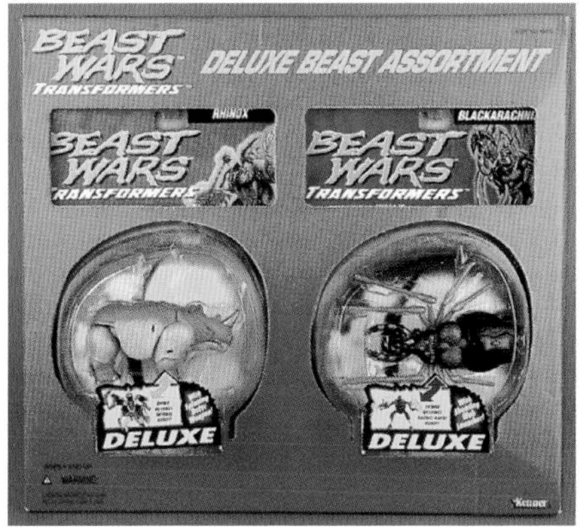

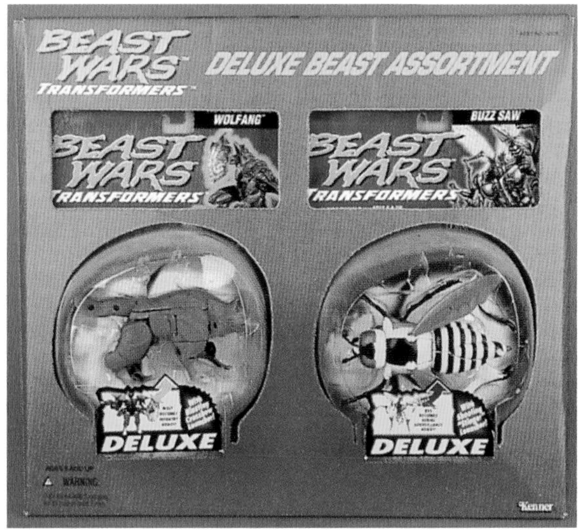

Rhinox with Blackarachnia and Wolfang with Buzz Saw

Botcon 1997 Convention Exclusive Fractyl and Packrat two-pack. *Courtesy of George Hubert*

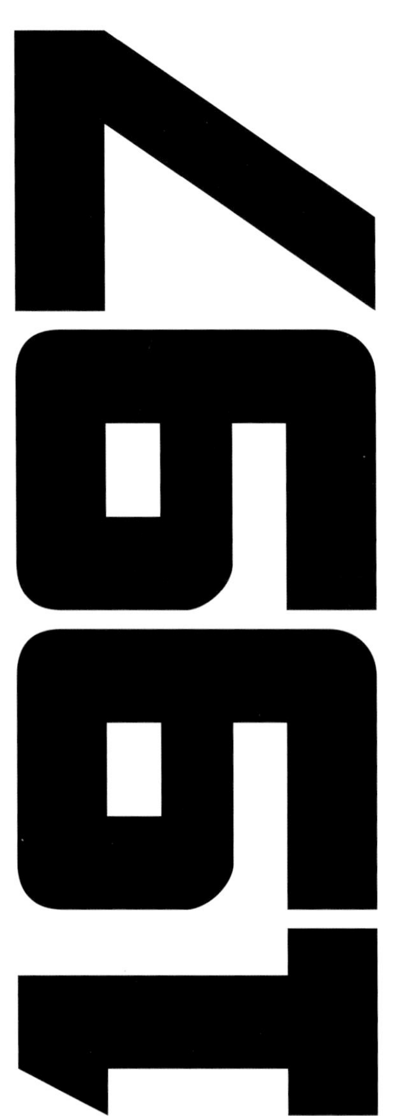

CHAPTER TEN

MACHINE WARS

In 1997, Hasbro tried to capitalize off the success of Beast Wars by reintroducing purely vehicular figures. Machine Wars brought back classic names and the original factions, the Autobots and Decepticons. This toy line was sold exclusively through Kay-Bee toys. The larger figures for this line were repaints of toys released by Hasbro during the gray area between the end of G1 and the beginning of G2. None of these larger figures had previously been released in North America. Being from an earlier era, they did not sport the articulation the Beast Wars figures were known for. The four new basic figures were inspired by Hasbro's other series and featured similar spring-loaded levers which would automatically transform or unfold the vehicle into robot mode. Unfortunately, it was not the right time and Machines Wars never made it past the first twelve figures.

MACHINE WARS CHECKLIST

Autobot Basic Machine Wars (Carded)
Hoist
Hubcap
Prowl
Mirage

Autobot Mega Machine Wars (Boxed)
Sandstorm

Autobot Ultra Machine Wars (Boxed)
Optimus Prime

Decepticon Basic Machine Wars (Carded)
Megatron
Megaplex
Skywarp
Thundercracker

Decepticon Mega Machine Wars (Boxed)
Soundwave

Decepticon Ultra Machine Wars (Boxed)
Starscream

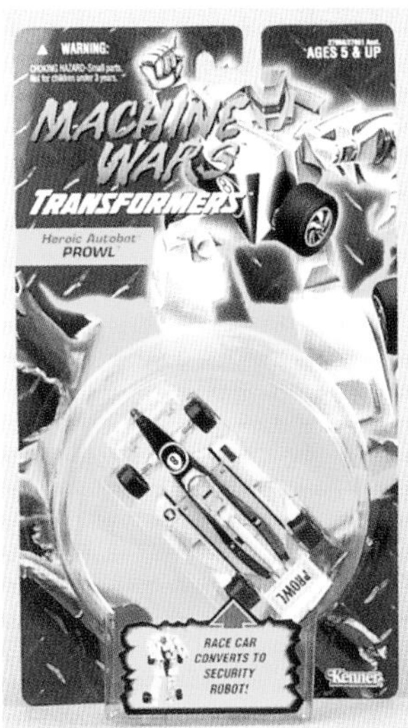

Prowl and Mirage. While the figures used classic Autobot names, the packaging actually reused card art from Generation 2 Jolt that was repainted and cropped.

Hubcap/Hoist and Skywarp/Thundercracker were the only figures from the line to receive new card/box art.

Megaplex and Megatron also reused card art from the Predator Falcon.

Mirage, Hubcap, Hoist, and Prowl. *Courtesy of Orson Christian of CapturedPrey.com*

Soundwave and Sandstorm were previously released as Stalker and Rotorstorm. Because of US safety laws, the small missiles and weapons that came with Stalker and Rotorstorm were left out of these versions.

Megatron, Megaplex, and Skywarp (Thundercracker shown in vehicle mode). *Courtesy of Orson Christian of CapturedPrey.com*

Soundwave and Sandstorm reused the box art for Stalker and Rotorstorm, albeit repainted.

Starscream was a repainted version of Skyquake. Again, due to safety concerns Starscream did not come with Skyquake's missile launching blasters.

Machine Wars figures are not terribly in demand on the secondary market. Starscream will sell anywhere from $30 to $50 sealed.

Machine Wars Optimus Prime was a repaint of European/Australian exclusive Thunder Clash. Slightly retooled from the Thunder Clash version, the trailer now came with spring-loaded missile launchers instead of the original reloading missiles.

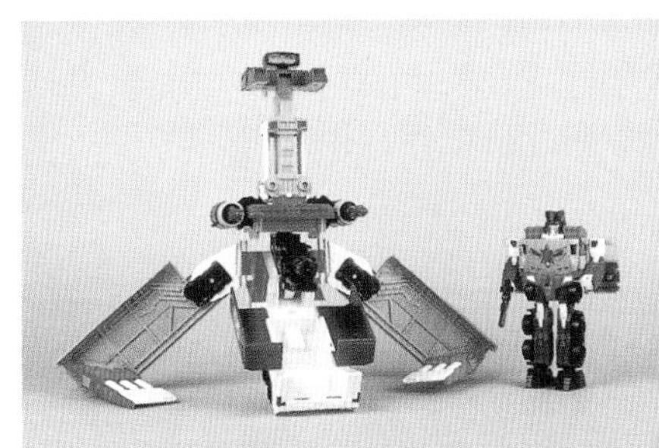

The Optimus Prime box featured a slightly modified reuse of the Generation 2 Laser Optimus Prime art.

CHAPTER ELEVEN

MERCHANDISE

Licensed goods are a staple of any worldwide mega brand. Here are some examples of licensed merchandise based off the Transformers brand.

The Jumbo Collectors Case was made of vinyl and had two shelves inside and a holding area for weapons.

This Collectors Case had a flimsy plastic tray inside for holding figures in place once the lid was closed.

The Collectors Showcase came with wires to tie figures down.

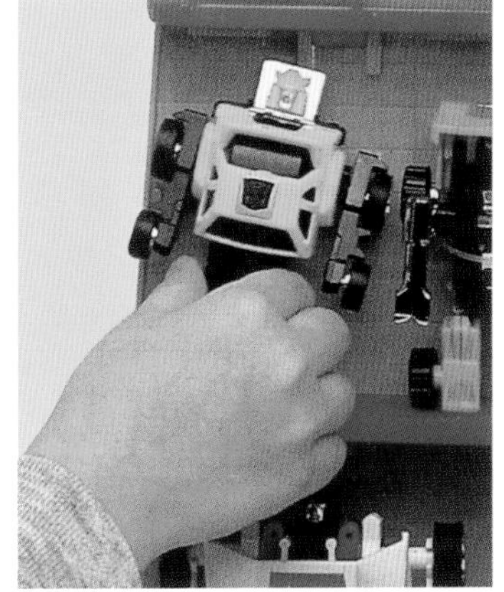

How interesting to see the rare yellow Cliffjumper on the box to the Showcase.

The Activity Center produced by Warren was made from cardboard. The bottom of the box needed to be used to form the actual playset. Sealed Activity Centers can sell for several hundred dollars.

Pinball Game

A staple of almost every show from the 1980s was having a board game.

Battlin' Robots inspired by the classic Rock'Em Sock'Em Robots. *Courtesy of Dan Hodkinson*

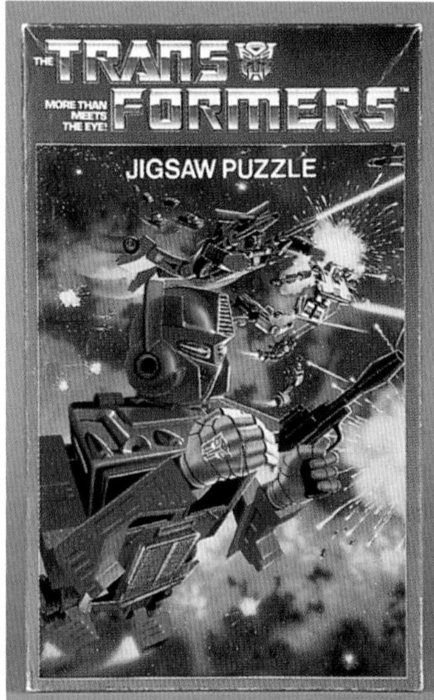

Warren also produced puzzles of different sizes.

The Action Cards consisted of a 192-card set featuring character box art and still frames from the television series.

Several 3-D jigsaw puzzles were produced by Warren, including Ultra Magnus, Starscream, and Bluestreak (shown). Each worked as a flat puzzle and as a 3-D puzzle for robot and vehicle mode.

Another Milton Bradley product was the four-player card game. *Courtesy of George Hubert*

Rik Alvarez—$15 to $25 on the secondary market.

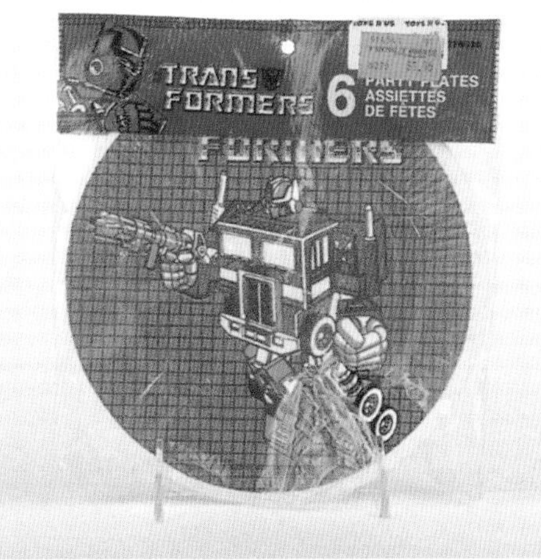

Large paper plates

Unique Party Industries produced numerous birthday supplies for the brand:

Accessory Pack with noise makers, centerpiece, loot bags, and hats

Party favor four-pack

Paper tablecloth cover

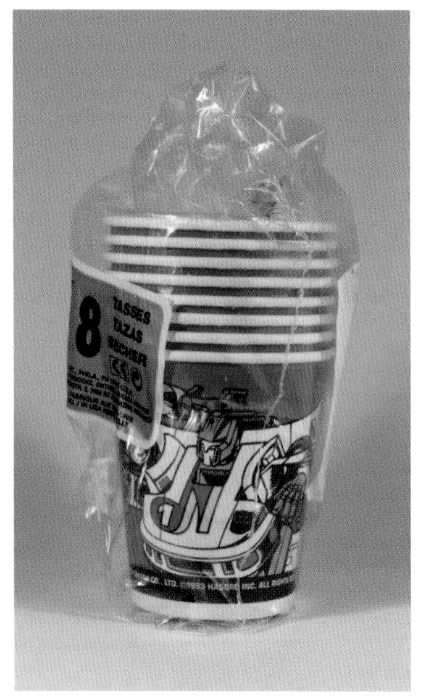

Even Generation 2 had party supplies

Loot Bags

The Desk Set produced by Creative Designs International had a pencil holder, two pencils, address book, writing area, paper pad, and a calendar for 1986 and 1987.

The set was made from vinyl. Shown are the two sides of the pencil holder.

Pencil toppers Optimus Prime and Megatron

Optimus Prime pencil sharpener next to Transformers pencils with toppers

An original vinyl pencil bag still sealed

These stamps were sold individually carded and in a gift set (shown, l to r): Jazz, Optimus Prime, Starscream, and Wheeljack.

The Snarl desk companion came with stamps, erasers, and pens. *Courtesy of George Hubert*

Individually carded Stamp Bots. *Courtesy of Ronen Kauffman of toylab.info*

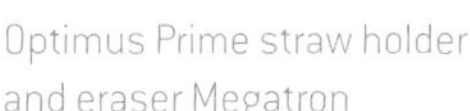

Optimus Prime straw holder and eraser Megatron

A small Starscream charm. *Courtesy of Dan Hodgkinson*

Jazz Stamper

Shirt Clip Ons of Wheeljack and Starscream. *Courtesy of George Hubert*

In addition to the comic books, Marvel also published many Transformers coloring books.

Plastic sunglasses. *Courtesy of Dan Hodgkinson*

Sticker Machine

Soundwave Design Center produced by Arrow

Pocket-sized Megatron puzzle

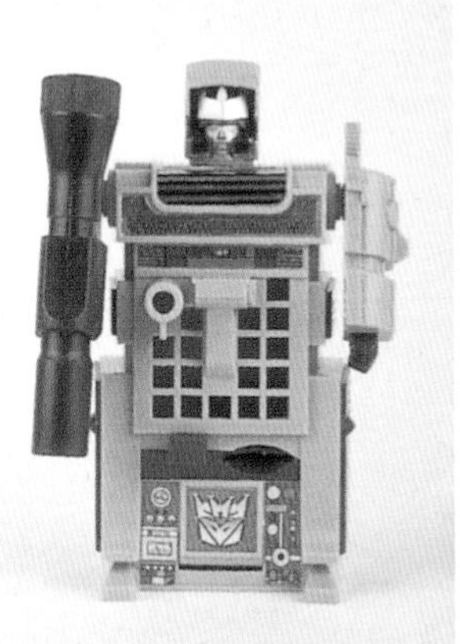

Megatron gumball machine

Coloring book published by Marvel.

Ravage wallet with lenticular image

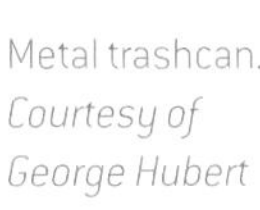

Metal trashcan. *Courtesy of George Hubert*

Decepto-Pack Dress Up set included a light-up blaster, chest plate, belt, shield, mask, and wrist cuffs. All the parts could be assembled into an uncomfortable backpack. *Courtesy of Dan Hodgkinson*

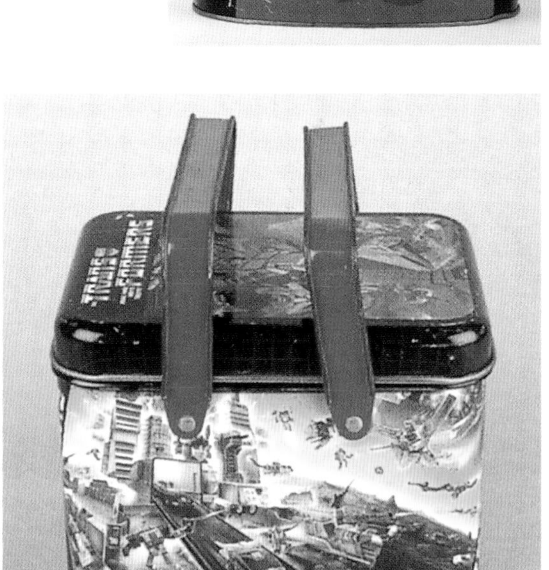

Small tin carrying case with removable lid

Carrying case—perfect for 45 RPM records.

Coloring book published by Marvel.

Styrofoam masks were even simpler and would just tie around a child's head. Shown is Silverbolt.

The Hide N Sleep tent could fit over any twin size mattress.

Collegeville Costumes are pure Americana; any child of the '70s and '80s wore one of their costumes at least one Halloween. Shown is Megatron. *Courtesy of George Hubert*

Collegeville made multiple costumes for the Transformers brand around characters such as Optimus Prime, Snarl, Silverbolt, and Ultra Magnus. This is the Superion mask.

Ultra Magnus voice changer

In the United Kingdom, Lets-B manufactured an Optimus Prime costume set. Almost identical to the Collegeville set, it came with a vinyl apron with the character's box art on it.

Bed sheets. *Courtesy of George Hubert*

Wallpaper.

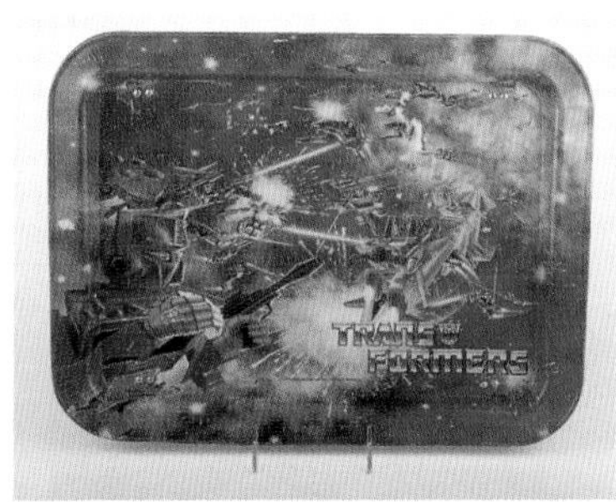

Metal bed trays featuring the back of package artwork from the 1984 and 1986 boxes. *Courtesy of George Hubert*

Aladdin manufactured several metal and plastic lunch boxes and thermoses. *Courtesy of George Hubert*

Roughneck produced lunch boxes with original art in the United Kingdom.

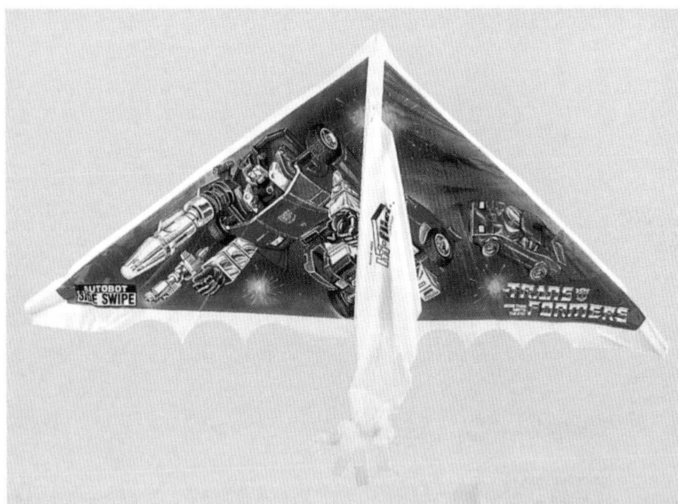

There were several kites from the Generation One era with Sideswipe (shown), Optimus Prime, and Kickback.

Generation 2 Galvatron flip-up character watch. *Courtesy of George Hubert*

Ziploc bags in-pack premium Rodimus Prime iron-on patch. *Courtesy of Dan Hodgkinson*

From the UK comes this foldout flyer made by Peter Pan Playthings.

Roller skates

An extremely hard-to-find item is the UK exclusive Jazz Peddle Car. A rather large item, this rare gem can sell between $350 and $450.

Sandbot could disassemble into a shovel, bucket, colander, and tray.

Another item from the UK, the Bath time Attack Pack. The Optimus Prime soap from the back was also sold individually.

Also from the Uk was this Optimus Prime Bubble Bath.

Also from overseas is the Thrust bubble maker.

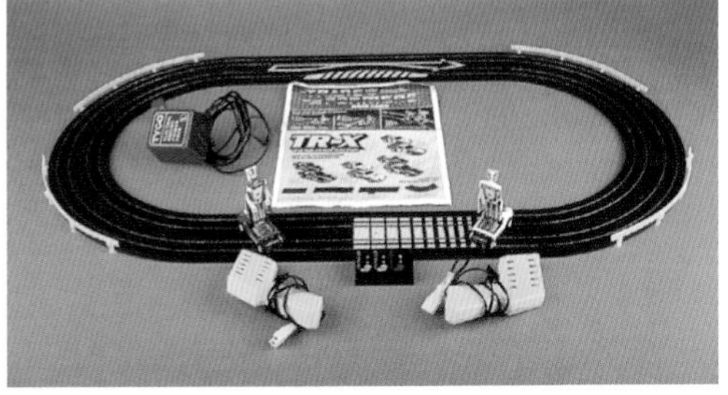

The Tyco-produced Electric Racing Set. The set came with transforming slot cars with Prowl and Rumble faces.

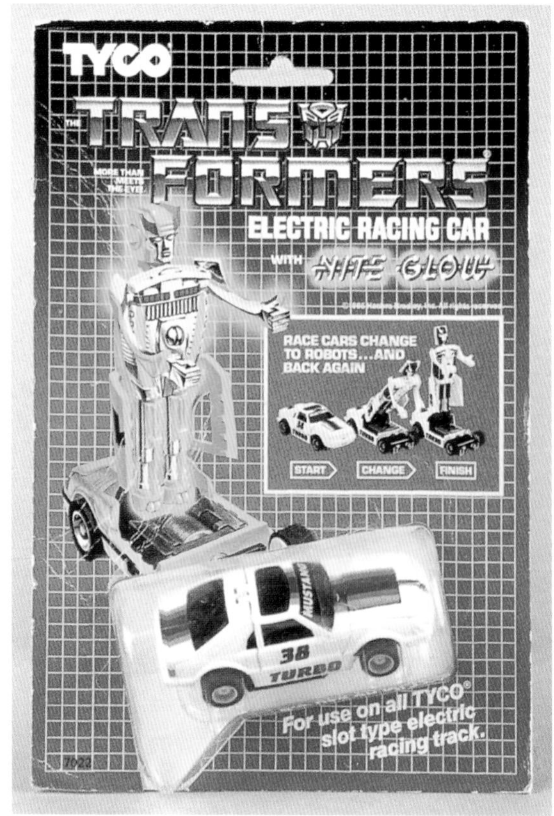

The glow-in-the-dark slot cars also came individually carded.

These slot cars will work on any standard Tyco slot car race set.

Another Tyco product was the Electric Train and Battle Set. The full set came with a massive fold out canvas, small plastic generic robots, and cardboard structures.

The Electronic Intercom Telephone System had a cord running from one walkie to another.

Coloring book published by Marvel.

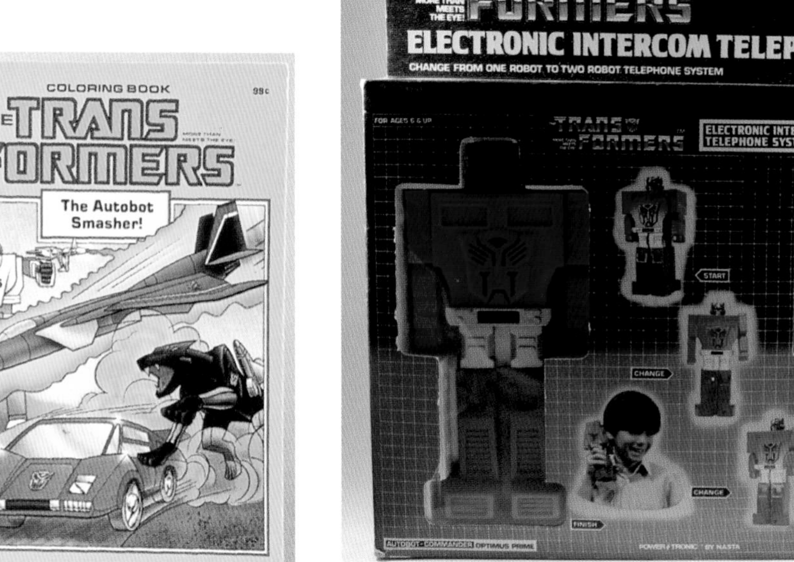

Autobot symbol AM Radio. The Autobot symbol was a facade that could flip open to reveal Optimus Prime's face.

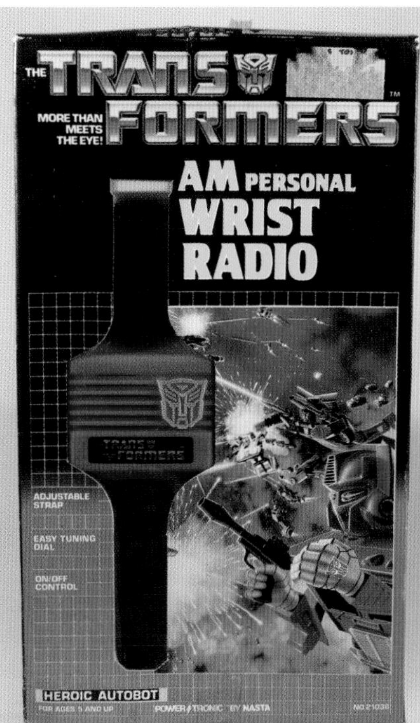

Wrist Radio

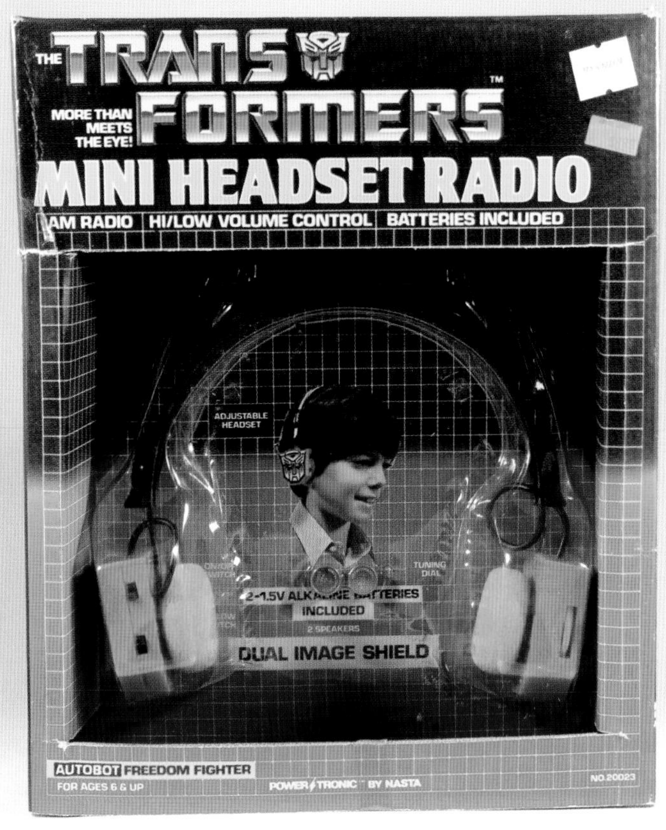

Mini Headset Radio

Optimus Prime AM radio. *Courtesy of Ronen Kauffman of toylab.info*

North American and Italian Frenzy radio released by GiG. *Courtesy of Ronen Kauffman of toylab.info*

Canadian Frenzy radio released by NASTA. This item was also released in the United States in an English only box.

View-Master Show Beam Projector. *Courtesy of George Hubert*

F.H.E. released several episodes on VHS.

Courtesy of George Hubert

View-Master slides

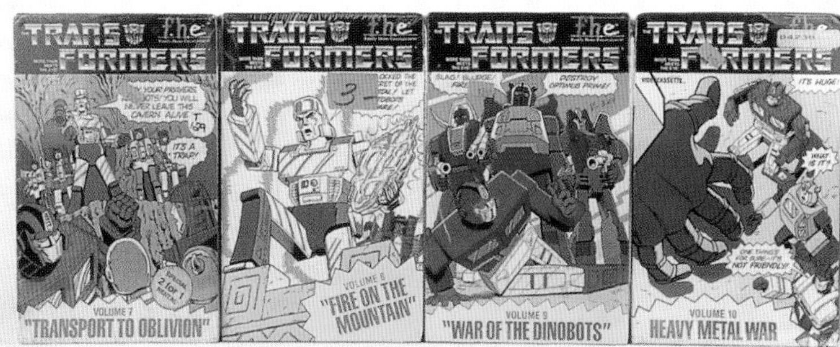

VHS tapes still sealed in these oversized boxes can range between $50 and $60. *Courtesy of George Hubert*

The Rebirth three-part episodes were the last Generation One episodes to air in North America.

Courtesy of George Hubert

These episodes were also released on regular-sized VHS tape boxes.

Transformers: The Movie

The Return of Optimus Prime two-part episodes were some of the few season three episodes released on VHS at the time.

A Canadian edition of the movie released during the mid-1990s. *Courtesy of George Hubert*

F.H.E. also released several episodes on Betamax. *Courtesy of Jim Black*

In 1989, Hill Crane released the Transformers film on Laserdisc in Japan. *Courtesy of Erik Nelson*

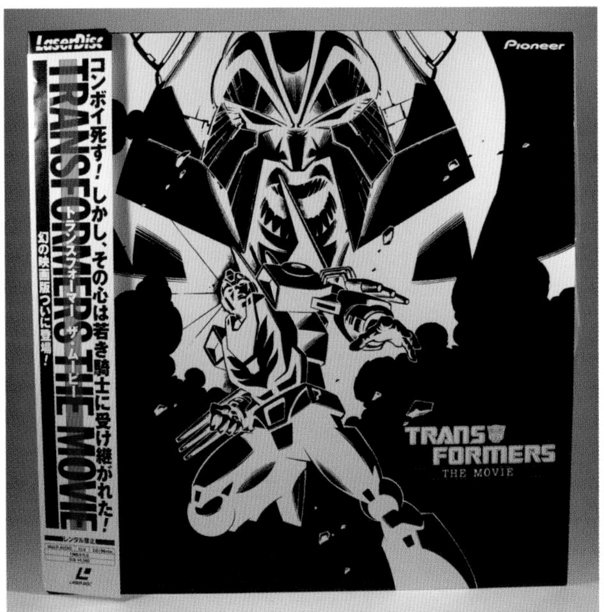

In 1998, this black and white sleeve edition of the film was released on Laserdisc. *Courtesy of Erik Nelson*

Some audiocassettes did not have companion books.

The soundtrack was later available on cassette and CD.

A curious item from Japan, the rarely seen V-01 video collection. This set came with character cards for everyone featured on the back of the box. The tape contains a twenty-minute clip show named *Transformers: The World* created from several episodes of Takara's *Headmasters* and *Super-God Masterforce* television series. *Courtesy of Chuck Liu of artfire2000.com*

The film's soundtrack was released on LP (a.k.a. a record). *Courtesy of Dan Hodgkinson*

Kids Stuff released several books with companion audiocassettes and LPs. *Courtesy of Dan Hodgkinson*

Another item from Japan was this spring-loaded gun with a target. Included in the set was a plastic Ultra Magnus.

The Satellite of Doom came with a 45 record.

In Japan, Decoys were also released in gift sets instead of being packed out randomly with individual figures. *Courtesy of George Hubert*

Takara also continued to produce new Decoys in several colors long after Hasbro ended their in-pack promotion. Seen here are Rodimus Prime, Metroplex, and Galvatron.

From Venezuela, this comic was a reprinting of the first issue produced by Marvel. It comes with English and Spanish text.

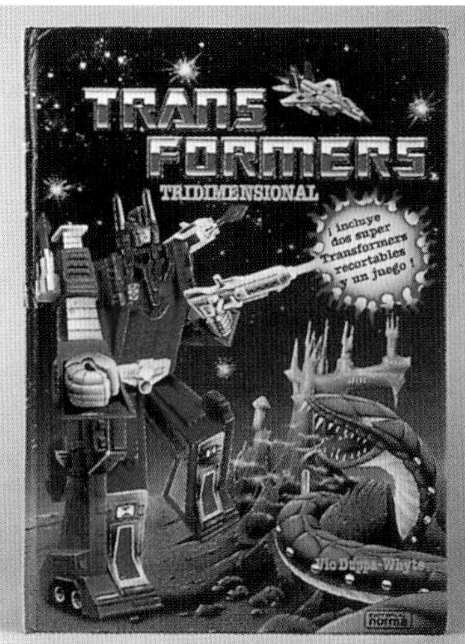

This pop-up book was printed in English and Spanish. It came with a transforming paper Starscream and an Ultra Magnus standee.

Ballantine Books published several choose-your-own-adventure books.

Often the Transformers would cross over with Action Force (a.k.a. G.I. Joe in North America). Next to it is a collection of several of the early comics. *Courtesy of George Hubert*

Examples of the British comics produced by Marvel. This series of comics split with the North American books' continuity and continued for several years with their own story lines. *Courtesy of George Hubert*

The first of the original Marvel run of comics.

Marvel also released small collected editions of the comics featuring several issues in one book.

Several three-to-four-issue series were published during its run. Shown is issue one of the movie adaptation.

G.I. Joe versus Transformers #1 took place within the continuity of both ongoing books.

The four-issue series of Transformers Universe featured bios and statistics for many of the characters.

Headmasters #1

The first issue of Generation 2. This book was also published by Marvel and lasted twelve issues.

The final issue of the original Transformers Marvel run. Initially this book was only going to last four issues, but due to its success it ran for eighty, which is why the top of the book says "#80 IN A FOUR-ISSUE LIMITED SERIES."

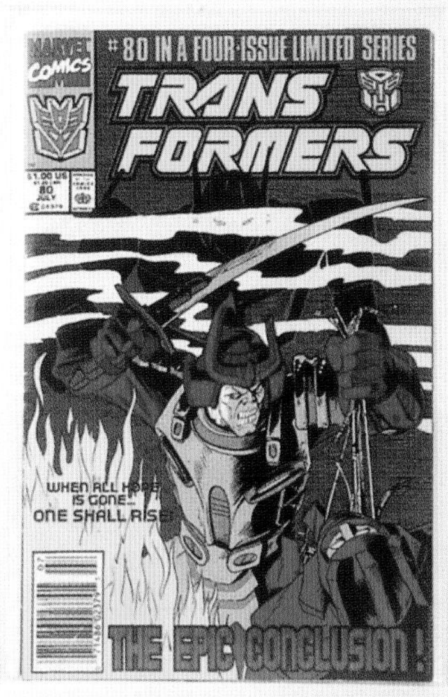

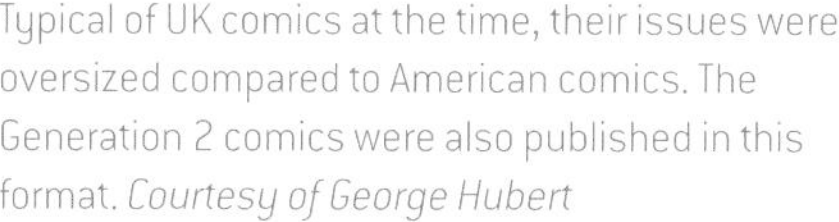
Typical of UK comics at the time, their issues were oversized compared to American comics. The Generation 2 comics were also published in this format. *Courtesy of George Hubert*

Generation 2 #8

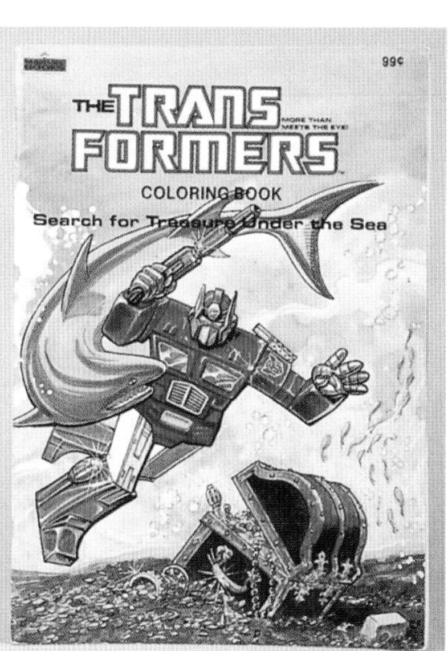

A Transformers brand cereal was also set to be produced, however only a handful of sample boxes were made for salesmen to use to promote with. This cereal would have also included the mail away Jazz figure incentive available with both Cookie Crisp and Cracker Jack cereals. *Courtesy of Shawn Fox*

Several puzzles were produced in 1991 for the Chinese markets featuring the original box art. These puzzles were most likely released to coincide with reissues being produced at the time.

A rare gem indeed, this is the mysterious Trailbreaker Power Cycle. It was produced by COLECO in 1984, in West Hartford, Connecticut. Power Cycles from this time period are generally extremely rare to find in good condition, let alone with the box. This unassembled sample with intact sticker sheet and instructions is easily worth between $1,800 and $2,000. *Courtesy of Shawn Fox*

As stated earlier, one of the great things about this brand is the ability to collect for thirty years and still be surprised at some of the items that seem to come out of nowhere. Seen here is the elusive beach pail. It features stylized box art of Omega Supreme, Blaster, and Ultra Magnus.